FRIEND TO FRIEND
Dogs That Help Mankind

This book is dedicated to

ROYAL

who in life taught me so much
about the companionship of dogs,
and in death led me to Morgan.

FRIEND TO FRIEND

Dogs That Help Mankind

by

CHARLOTTE SCHWARTZ

Foreword by Roger Caras

FIRST EDITION
1984

HOWELL BOOK HOUSE INC.
230 Park Avenue
New York, N.Y. 10169

Library of Congress Cataloging in Publication Data

Schwartz, Charlotte.
Friend to friend.

1. Working dogs. I. Title.
SF428.2.S39 1985 636.7 84-19233

ISBN 0-87605-545-5

Printed in the U.S.A.

Contents

FRIEND TO FRIEND
Dogs That Help Mankind

The author, Charlotte Schwartz, and her German Shepherd Dog, Morgan.

About the Author

CHARLOTTE SCHWARTZ'S credentials are awe-inspiring. My first introduction to this remarkable lady came at the Dog Fanciers Club on March 10, 1982 when she spoke on *The New Role of the Dog in the Space Age.* Her presentation was so warm, so worthy and promising to the millions of unfortunate folks whose lives are now being enhanced by the human-dog bond that I asked her to write this book.

Charlotte has served as Chairman of the Education and Training Committee of the National Association of Dog Obedience Instructors. She is founder and chief instructor of the Brandy Lane Farm Dog Training School, one of America's leading obedience schools with 50 full-time members. The school's "pupils" have amassed over 100 obedience titles and tracking degrees.

She is a writer with frequent contributions to the *American Kennel Gazette,* the official publication of the American Kennel Club, *Off-Lead Magazine* and the NADOI *News.* The Philadelphia Police K-9 Corps has awarded her Certificates of Appreciation. Charlotte has served as Advisor to the Newfoundland Water Rescue dog trainers, and developed special programs for messenger dogs, back-packing dogs, guard dogs and dogs to assist the handicapped.

As a member of the Delta Society, which is devoted to research, education and service on the interactions of people, animals and the environment, she attended an International Symposium on the Human/Pet Relationship honoring the eightieth birthday of Nobel Prize Winner, Prof. Konrad Lorenz, in October 1983.

Charlotte is a dynamic speaker, humorous, entertaining and knowledgeable. She can solve almost any dog problem.

To the millions of handicapped, infirm and lonely men, women and children this book will bring aid, hope and courage.

—ELSWORTH HOWELL

Foreword

by Roger Caras

AS SOMEONE who grew up with dogs all around him, I am always somewhat amazed (I am too old to be totally amazed by anything) that there are still people who don't know the many ways in which their own lives have been enriched by dogs.

Even if you don't own a dog and never have you may have not been blown up by a bomb in the cargo hold of a jetliner because a bomb dog, without your knowledge, discovered an explosive device put there by a maniac. Far-fetched? Hardly, since there is a school for bomb dogs. A lot of drugs, an awful lot of drugs never reach the streets of the town or city where you live because drug dogs sniffed them out and customs made yet another dog-guided seizure. Far-fetched? There is a school for drug detection dogs, too. Both schools are run by the federal government.

People denied of sight are guided through life by dogs, there are hearing-ear dogs, but all of this the general reader probably knows. Perhaps fewer people lucky enough to pick up this delightful volume of anecdote, lore, insight and joy will know about the health aspects, the psychological healing and other canine focused enrichments of the human condition.

Thank heavens there is a Charlotte Schwartz, woman of wit and wisdom, to bring all of this together. The only thing more important than having Charlotte Schwartz to write this book is that there have been dogs for her to write about.

Ms. Schwartz is a woman not wanting for courage. She dares draw conclusions and although I can't honestly say that every last one of them is a new kind of gospel she is a wise person and nothing she says can be dismissed. There is far more than anecdote here, there is penetration. What gets penetrated? The mists of time, adventure and misadventure. Dogs have been around longer than marriage, income tax and the other immortal forces in our lives, perhaps as long as a couple of hundred centuries, and if you want to speculate on the events of that span of time you had better be prepared to dig and penetrate and make some educated guesses. Charlotte Schwartz doesn't blanch before the task. She wades in, sorts it out, and tells it as she sees it. She is my kind of dog-loving writer.

A lot of writers about dogs are timid. There is a body of safe data that can be drawn upon and restated (research, I think they call it) and if you are careful no other writers or critics or dog-lovers will get angry. (It is very hard to write about dogs without making people angry because dog-lovers are emotional hypochondriacs and are sure you are out to hurt dogs when you even use the word "d . . .".) Ms. Schwartz is not timid. She never gets silly and flies off at weird tangents but she obviously studies and studies and examines and discusses and then offers the not inconsiderable benefit of her insight.

I am very pleased that I was asked to write the Foreword to this grand, informative book not just because the assignment will make me immensely wealthy, but because I care about what Charlotte Schwartz (someday we will meet and I will call her Charlotte, but not here in print) has done, about the facts and the meanings of those facts that she has assembled and written about with style and purpose and tone. I am angry that I didn't write this book and she didn't do the Foreword, but those are the breaks. In the meantime, as you leave this page behind (as well you should) and move ahead, enjoy, learn, but above all appreciate the miracle we have at our hearts' disposal. Lord love our dogs and protect writers like Charlotte Schwartz who writes so exceedingly well about them.

ROGER CARAS, East Hampton

Editor's Note: Mr. Caras has written his own book about dogs, A CELEBRATION OF DOGS, and has no earthly right to be angry that he didn't write this book, too.

Author's Preface

THANKS TO THE PATIENT TEACHINGS of my father when I was a child, I have always respected the fragile union of man and animals. I was raised for a good many years on a farm, and it was there I learned to love both the animals and the people who cared for them.

Today I am a teacher by profession and I particularly enjoy sharing what I have learned with others. Because of my love for dogs and people, I want to help improve the quality of life for both.

When the idea for this book surfaced, I began writing letters to everyone I knew. I asked them to tell me of their experiences with their dogs. I wanted to hear about dogs working with and helping people, and how the dogs had affected those lives.

Most of them answered. And they also told me about other people. People who are sick and disabled. People who fight the darkness and the loneliness and the silence with the help of dogs. Then I contacted those people myself.

I prowled the halls of libraries and read dozens of books. I researched the history of dogs and mankind. I asked questions of everyone I met, and I listened. I listened and remembered and came rushing home to record what I heard.

Each chapter told the true-life story of dogs helping mankind. Whether that help came in the form of therapy or a dog working for its master, I told the story as I learned it. Each new chapter emerged more exciting than the one before.

Through all the stories ran a thread that, however one chooses to explain it, documents the bond between dogs and mankind.

I thought of the wonderful painting by Sir Edwin Landseer called "Attachment." It depicts a little terrier guarding the body of his dead master on a storm-swept crag. In grand Victorian style, it reminds the viewer of the strength of that invisible bond.

I have divided the man/dog relationship into three categories: A Historical Perspective, Therapy Dogs and Service Dogs. And for those who seek a challenge, there's even a final section on jobs for dogs in the future.

For my story to help the greatest number of people, I have compiled a directory at the back of the book. Anyone wishing additional information on any category of the man/dog relationship can find it in the directory.

Throughout the writing there have been many people who gave graciously of themselves so I could tell the story of dogs helping mankind. Debby Parlini did all the typing and organized the research material; Ken Parlini spent hours taking photographs and traveling to get them printed exactly the way I wanted them; Pat Hoster relieved me of many responsibilities at Brandy Lane Farm so I could find the time to write; special friends gave their loving support: Nancy, Georgie, Sue, Tilly and Irwin. Marion Hilpert, Linda Hines, Hugh H. Tebault, Drs. Leo K. Bustad, James J. Lynch and Alan M. Beck all helped with the research. I owe a special debt to the people who told me their stories and shared their experiences, sometimes their innermost thoughts and feelings.

And finally Joe, my husband of thirty years, who has suffered, mostly in silence, as I neglected things that otherwise I would have done in and around our home. To all of them, I send my most sincere thanks.

This is the Age of Science, a century of mechanization. Now it is time to take these man-made marvels and unite them with the innate abilities of the dog to create better lives for all of us.

For perhaps, if the truth were known, we're all a little blind, a little deaf, a little handicapped, a little lonely, a little less than perfect. And if we can learn to appreciate and utilize the dog's full potentials, we will, together, make it in this life on earth.

Charlotte Schwartz
Mt. Holly, N.J.

PART I

A Historical Perspective

In the Beginning

As the children nestled down in the soft fur of their sleeping place and the night wrapped its darkness around them, they heard the cries again. At first, they were soft cries, almost whimpers, like the halfhearted protests of one puppy nudging another in its sleep. But soon, the cries grew stronger and more pleading and, since an episode such as this had happened several hot suns ago, the children knew they would not cease. The crying would grow in intensity until the dark and the cold silenced forever the tiny creatures who called so helplessly now for the mother who would never return to them.

The children knew where the nest was hidden. They had seen the she-dog several times as she left the pups in their cave to join the dog and her pack. They had watched from a nearby streambank as the she-dog returned to feed her three babies after the hunt. As circumstances would have it, they had, this day, seen the mother dog leave with her tall, gray mate and head out across the meadow to join the others in an afternoon foray.

When the sun dipped below the treetops, the children went back to their own fire and promptly forgot the activities of the canid family. It wasn't until they heard the whimpering in the dark that they recalled the incident at all. Immediately, they realized the pups were crying because the she-dog had failed to return. And they knew, this time, they would not let the puppies die. They would go to the den and bring the young canids back to their site where they would care for them and ultimately play with them as they grew stronger.

. . . .

This vignette might well be the way it was in the beginning when man and dog made the first unspoken pact to live together and be friends and companions. The children were the get of a prehistoric man and the dogs were of the wild canid. Both were wise in the ways of the other and cunning in the ways of self-survival.

This awareness of each other had begun many, perhaps hundreds, of years before. Like most species fourteen thousand years ago, primitive man was probably both the hunter and the hunted. So it was, also, for the wolf-like wild dog that roamed the land in packs. In sharing the environment with each other, man and wild dog slowly learned there were definite advantages to be had from observing each others' behavior and staying close to one another.

At night, for instance, the dogs stationed themselves just beyond the firelight of man and waited for him to discard unwanted food bits. No doubt they took notice when he moved his campsite to more prolific hunting grounds and better water holes. The urge to prepare for worsening weather and threatening storms was also probably noted and acted upon by the dogs.

In return, man paid attention when the dogs warned of approaching predators or their keenness of smell foretold of nearby game. Man must have noticed how easily the dogs picked up the slightest movement in the bush and used this early warning signal to his own advantage.

Eventually, dogs joined man in the hunt for food and the defense of his home and family because the two species had learned the benefits of this mutual relationship. So it was inevitable that the get of primitive man should join together with the get of the wild dog to form the first bond between the two species. This relationship has evolved to a state of such sophistication that, today, man and dog claim the closest relationship of any two species ever to walk the earth together.

EARLY DAYS

There are no books to tell us exactly when dogs emerged as true companions of man, but drawings from primitive caves dating back to the ancient civilizations of Egypt show dogs hunting with man and horses. Falconers often used dogs to retrieve the prey brought down by their birds, and the tomb of Tutankhamen was guarded by a statue of an Ibizan Hound named Anubis.

In Europe and the Far East, dogs accompanied kings on their journeys and guarded their flocks in the fields. Very small dogs were bred as playthings for Oriental ladies. Archeologists have unearthed the bones of dogs that died with their masters in volcanic eruptions.

So, from the Java man whose dwelling was a cave through the period when great nomadic tribes wandered the earth to the day when man built crude cabins and began to till the soil, he has been accompanied by his friend and helper, the dog.

As the process of evolution continued, man began to refine the dog through controlled breeding to fit his various needs. He bred the alert, aggressive ones to guard his campsite against marauding tribes and errant wanderers. He fashioned hunting companions from the genes of dogs that possessed keenness of smell and sight, the soft, gentle companions were for his family to enjoy. Whatever the direction man's simple methods of animal husbandry took on, the dog's qualities of love, intelligence and fidelity always emerged as his most endearing traits. The ultimate outcome was the total devotion dogs have pledged to man and the responsibility man has assumed in accepting that devotion.

THE CIVILIZATION OF MAN AND DOG

With the development of civilization, man took up one of two roles: he became a follower, a worker; or he became a leader, often a wealthy landowner and sometimes a member of royalty. In both cases, dog served man willingly. Workers maintained dogs for their help in draft work and guarding, and as ratters, hunters and herders. Royalty, on the other hand, kept dogs for personal hunting, guarding, companionship and for entertainment such as racing and fighting.

The further development of civilization forced man into community living. Thus, cities and countries were formed. Once again, dogs changed with man. More breeds were developed to suit the new lifestyles. For the first time, miniaturization through selective breeding became a common practice. Small dogs made excellent pets and proved easier to maintain in the new, more highly populated environments.

By the time modern man was established, dogs were used primarily as companion-pets. Although a small percentage still served man as guards, messengers, hunters, retrievers, herders and leaders of the blind, yet another need began to emerge. More breeds were developed and improved to suit the tastes of those seeking elegance, dependence and uniqueness. Dogs became the companions of the masses and the status symbols of the wealthy.

This is where the man/dog relationship remained for many decades. Some dogs were pets, some worked, some were status symbols. Whatever his function, the dog had proved by his adaptability that he was here to stay.

Now the cycle of time has once again brought man and dog into a newer, more exciting relationship than ever before in the history of the two species. Through research in ethology, genetics and psychology, dogs are assuming an even more important role in the lives of man in the Space Age. It is indeed a renaissance, a new birth of an age-old kinship.

The Sport of Dogs Today

Any discussion or definitive work detailing how dogs improve the quality of life for mankind would be incomplete and inappropriate if some mention was not made of how dogs participate in activities that bring pleasure, companionship, personal reward and achievements to their owners. In modern times people, young and old, male and female, athletic and not-so-athletic, can and do participate in a wide variety of activities with dogs.

Some of the activities are based on behaviors for which the dogs were initially bred. Others are man-developed to provide fun for dog and master. Regardless, the participants are as dedicated and enthusiastic as any other group of sports buffs the world over. And, because their partners are animals, most demonstrate more creativity and grit than people who fancy sports involving mere objects.

Before one can participate in a sport with a dog, one must train the dog. Sometimes that training can involve hours of practice, a great deal of money and miles of travel. Whatever, the triumph of success is even headier when one achieves a goal with an unpredictable, four-legged partner.

The pure pleasure of companionship that a dog brings to any relationship with mankind is enough for some. The idea that a dog is a nonjudgmental, devoted friend, always waiting, always grateful, always faithful is probably the most abiding reason for choosing a dog as a companion. Yet there are those who choose to go a step beyond—to take the dog a step above his station of companionship to some academic feat.

The reasons for choosing a dog sport can be as varied as the people and dogs who participate in them. Prime among them would be the pleasure a dog owner receives from witnessing his

A classic example of companionship—a boy and his dog. *Charlotte Schwartz*

Here the same boy and dog become involved in the hobby of dog obedience. They will learn to work as a team and attend dog shows.
Charlotte Schwartz

canine partner learn a new behavior and perform it. Next, there are those among us who are born competitors. They want a dog who can compete as fiercely as they do.

Man's ego is another reason some train their dogs to perform certain behaviors. It brings them recognition and they receive great satisfaction from being noticed and admired.

Then, there are the purists. They are the people who develop latent talents within the dog and delight in seeing this ability resurface. Sometimes the activity is harmless and exciting to watch. Other times it is cruel and inhumane. Take, for example, lure coursing. Sight hounds, who for centuries raced across the desert to catch their quarry, are once again participating in the hunt. Only this time the quarry is a plastic rabbit, but the chase is just as exciting for people and dogs as it was three thousand years ago.

Dog-fighting is an example of some men's passion for excitement at the expense of another living being. The fact that the fighting itself and the related gambling is illegal is little reason for them to abstain.

Perhaps the most positive result of dog sports, aside from raising more talented dogs, is the intangible element of personal development and self-actualization realized by the people involved. The effort and reward of nurturing a dog brings a love so constant it can help mankind develop its inner self.

Listed below are just some of the many sports involving dogs. Anyone wishing to become involved in them can obtain additional information by contacting local kennel clubs and the American Kennel Club whose address is listed in the Directory.

Breed Competition. Soundness of body and mind are demonstrated by dogs entered at dog shows. The dogs, both male and female, must be breedable and as near to the standard of perfection for their breed as possible. There are dog shows throughout the year all across the country. Winners at breed shows are on their way to becoming breed champions and are usually the stock from which future generations will come.

Obedience Competition. Again, soundness of body and mind is necessary, but in addition the quality of trainability is demanded at these events. There are various levels of accomplishment that are recognized by titles such as

Companion Dog, Companion Dog Excellent and Utility Dog. An Obedience Trial Champion is a dog that has excelled at all levels and met the American Kennel Club's most rigorous standards of performance.

Tracking Trials. Here dogs exhibit their ability to follow the path of someone who has gone ahead of them minutes or hours before. These tests are usually conducted in large rural areas where dogs lead their handlers to a dropped article that the track-layer has left behind. Dogs that have passed tracking tests have the letters T.D. placed after their registered names.

Field Trials. There are many kinds of field trials, some recognized by the American Kennel Club, others recognized by specific breed clubs only. In all these tests dogs are expected to perform the behavior for which they were bred. For example, spaniels, setters and pointers flush and retrieve upland game for their masters.

Retrievers bring back fallen water fowl for the hunter and are awarded various titles for the level of achievement they demonstrate.

Terriers and Dachshunds "go to ground" to flush out varmint, such as ground hog and ferret, and are awarded certificates attesting to their level of gameness.

Dog Sledding. Here dogs are trained singly or in teams to pull sleds carrying people and cargo. Races are held each year to determine the teams with the most stamina and strength to perform the task for which they were originally bred.

Back-packing. One dog, one master set out across open fields or thick forest to experience the wonder of nature and the thrill of being alone in the wild. The dog carries a back-pack containing his own food and supplies for his master. A trip can last an hour or a month, yet it brings the two together in an awareness of each other that becomes a living bond.

Scent Hurdle Racing. Here's a fun activity that requires several dogs and handlers, some low hurdles and a scented article such as a wooden dumbbell for each dog. It brings out the fun of competition, the laughs of great goofs and an excitement for all not unlike a child's first visit to a circus. This is always a big crowd pleaser at dog shows, country fairs and canine demonstrations.

Exhibition Teams. Kennel clubs and dog training schools throughout the world are frequently involved in giving demonstrations to show the public what dogs can do. These teams perform individual behaviors as well as highly complicated precision routines that make every spectator want to go home and train his own dog. And, in the doing, everyone has a good time.

Exhibition teams are also discussed in the chapters on pet-facilitated therapy. They are being recognized more and more as the catalysts in the study of the human companion animal bond.

Schutzhund. This is a sport for owners of working dogs. The name Schutzhund is a German word meaning protection dog. In this sport, dog and owner perfect three categories of the working dog's natural instincts: tracking, obedience and protection. They attend Schutzhund trials to demonstrate this perfection and are awarded titles for various levels of achievement.

Stock Dog Trials. At these events owners of working stock dogs compete for scores and recognition from their peers as well as offer their dogs an opportunity to exercise their natural instincts. The owner guides the dog in rounding up cattle, sheep or ducks to demonstrate the dog's herding ability—just as he's been doing for thousands of years. The All Breed Trial Association sponsors these events every year across the country.

Water Rescue Trials. In this activity dogs are being trained to revive natural instincts. Newfoundlands in particular are once again being given the opportunity to rescue "drowning" victims and objects. The tests are conducted at water sites and the dogs who perform successfully are awarded various titles to indicate their level of achievement.

True to the meaning of the word "sport," these and many other dog activities are creating a diversion for both dog and mankind that brings pleasure to all who engage in them. There seems little chance that they will die out in the years to come.

PART II

Therapy Dogs

Just keep stroking. I love it! *The Latham Foundation*

Dogs and the Aged

The rising and receding tides of time had etched deep rivulets in the old man's face. His hands wore the leathered look of almost a hundred summer suns and Minnesota winters. The stoop of his back bore mute testimony to his years of working the land, tilling the soil and reaping the harvests for his fellow man.

Now he was put out to pasture in the sterile green field of a home for the aged. But his mind was not ready to quit. Unable to find stimulation in his new surroundings, he retreated to the memories of the past.

Silently he passed the days. From his window he observed the coming and going of yet another year. Always silent, always reflective, always lonely.

Then one day a young woman brought a little white mixed breed dog to visit him. At first he smiled, his hands hesitating lest the wagging tail and licking tongue be snatched from him. Then the years of busyness and the animals in his life came flooding back.

The old man reached out a hand and touched the silken mane and warm body beneath. His heart raced and his eyes sparkled as the little dog responded to his approach.

The dog was sitting on his lap now, and for the moment, times were good again. There was life and love in the world still. And they celebrated the moment together.

. . . .

It was a sunny day, July hot, with a soft breeze blowing across the manicured emerald lawn. The tall pines at the edge of the rose garden moved in slow motion and the frilled trim of the red and white awning fluttered just enough to keep those below it awake. If the people under the tent hadn't been in wheelchairs and on stretchers one would have thought it a rather routine garden party in an exclusive part of any town, U.S.A.

But the guests made it different. They were residents of the Presbyterian Home in Broomal, Pennsylvania. Men and women, they were all witnesses to life eighty to a hundred years ago. Most of them could recall those early days and some even talked about them. Others chose not to.

All felt the loneliness that comes when one is tucked away in the neat, sterile slot of a home for the aged, far from loved ones, removed from the mainstream of community life and isolated from the friends they had known and worked with most of their adult lives.

Across the Delaware River, in Clarksboro, New Jersey, a similar group gathered around picnic tables and consumed hamburgers, potato salad and gallons of iced tea as if they were kids again. They laughed and spilled their tea and got catsup on their faces and swatted flies just as they had done as children. This day, for a few hours, they were children again. Happy, carefree, loving and loved. Their eyes sparkled and, though their hands shook and their voices quivered now, they were alert and inquisitive, asking a million questions, sharing a thousand memories, feeling a hundred human emotions that had lain dormant too long.

The reason for the garden party in Pennsylvania and the picnic in New Jersey was that a small, but enthusiastic, band of dogs and dog owners chose to share a few precious hours with the aged. Some of the dogs did tricks to entertain them. Others performed obedience routines to demonstrate their intelligence. A few came just because they like people. All were there because their owners were members of K-9 Capers Exhibition Team at Brandy Lane Dog Training School in Mount Holly, New Jersey.

K-9 Capers and dozens of similar teams across the country are dedicated to sharing time with the elderly and teaching responsible pet ownership to the young. These groups work without pay under some of the most absurd conditions imaginable. I remember, for example, one home we went to had planned on having us perform on their spacious front lawn. However, as we arrived, the heavens dumped tons of rain on the area and we had to hustle dogs, handlers, equipment and old people back indoors.

Undaunted, we improvised the show in an area about ten feet square with wheelchairs, rolling cots and crutches bordering the show ring. Several of the more ambitious acts had to be changed or dropped from the program, but the audience didn't seem to mind. To them, it mattered most that we were there and times were good again.

In another incident, we performed in the rain while the old people watched from the windows of their air-conditioned dining room. Still another show took place in the middle of the living room of a country farmhouse because the home was a very small one with no large facility for entertaining and the weather was too cold to go outdoors.

But for every show, wherever it's held or whatever the contents of the program, the best part of the visit comes after the finale. That's when dogs and handlers mingle with the audience. That's when people get to touch other people and, most of all, the dogs. And it's when all the memories of long-forgotten pets come flooding back to be remembered and related.

A smile creeps across the face of an octogenarian who wants to pet a German Shepherd and tell the listener about the dog he once owned. The little lady in a blue sweater recalls how this blond Cocker Spaniel looks just like her old Buffy, now dead more than twenty years. A tall, thin man in a walker, now a shadow of the strapping big farmer he once was, tells about the Shelties and Border Collies he used a lifetime ago to herd his flocks on a farm in the Pennsylvania Dutch farmland. And as he recalls them, the tears fill his eyes with sadness and the listener looks discreetly away.

The most thrilling moment I ever witnessed happened in Pennsylvania. A tiny wisp of a woman, perhaps eighty-five or ninety, sat without saying a word to anyone throughout the show and the reception of tea and cookies that followed. No one spoke to her and she seemed not to have anything to say to others. A white-clad nurse had pushed her wheelchair to a spot in the front row before the show and there she stayed until the end. While everyone was enjoying the refreshments after the show, she sat silently watching the dogs as they mingled with the elderly. She asked no questions, petted no dog and no one seemed to even notice her.

Then one of the handlers and a dog, a large black Standard Poodle, deliberately stopped in front of her and began talking. Slowly she reached out a tiny, frail hand to pet the fluffy topknot of the dog. The dog looked up at her and licked her hand. The old lady smiled cautiously and, in a weak trill of a voice, said, "You have a beautiful face. What's your name?"

The dog's owner said, "Her name is Bonnie," and the old lady repeated the name aloud as she continued to pet the dog. The dog loved the attention and stood perfectly still, tail wagging, as the lady continued to talk to her. She told Bonnie she'd had several poodles in her life, each more treasured than the one before, each more intelligent than any other dog in the neighborhood, each as lovely as the one here before her.

As the visit progressed, it became obvious that she had no intention of speaking to the dog's owner. She seemed quite satisfied to have the undivided attention of such a regal animal, and felt no need to communicate with another human being.

The visit lasted for perhaps ten minutes, the dog's owner standing quietly in the background as the lady and the big dog shared the precious moment of togetherness as if they were apart from the crowd and the noise of the party. Then, as unexpectedly as it had begun, the encounter was over. The lady caressed the dog one more time and said, "I have to go now. Please come back." An attendant had arrived to take her back to her room and her solitude.

As I turned, for I was the handler and Bonnie was my dog, a rather well groomed lady of perhaps fifty approached me and asked, "I saw you talking to the little lady in the wheelchair. What did she say to you?"

I explained that she never did talk to me, only to Bonnie and only about her own poodles when she was younger and had a family of her own. The lady's eyes filled with tears, she dabbed at them with a white, lacy handkerchief and proceeded to tell me the story of her mother, the little old lady.

Her mother had suffered a stroke four years before and had never spoken a word since then. Although she'd had the best treatment and care money could buy, it seemed she would never talk again, even though the doctors kept saying they thought

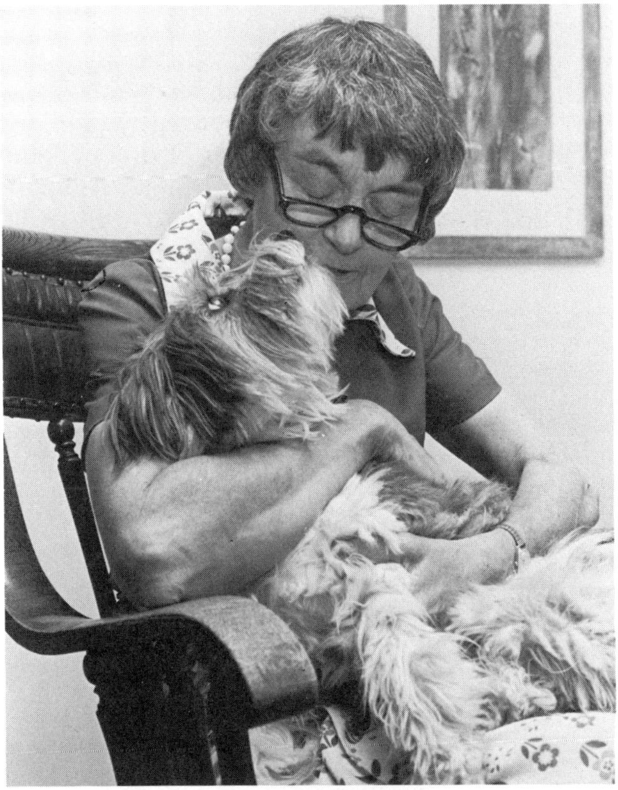

A soft, warm body helps a patient fight the loneliness.
The Latham Foundation

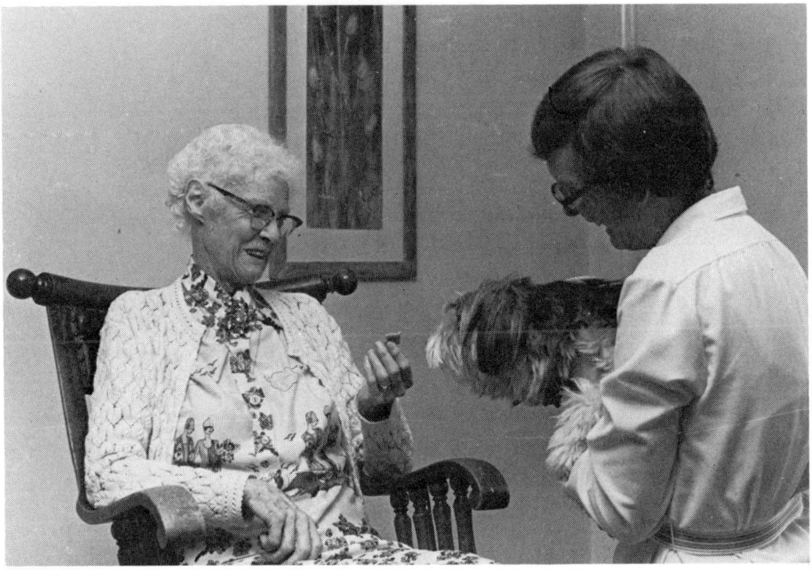

A treat makes an introduction more successful. *The Latham Foundation*

she could talk. No one seemed able to figure out the reason why she chose not to talk despite hours of therapy.

Following her stroke and the subsequent hospital stay, she had been placed in this exclusive home for the aged so that she could receive the best nursing care. All manner of therapy had been provided her, yet she did not respond. She remained silent and, after several years, it was decided that she would truly never talk again. And she didn't . . . until that afternoon in the garden.

Perhaps she chose to speak to Bonnie because she saw the dog as a friend, loving and nonjudgmental. One of the doctors and the lady's daughter had seen her talking to the dog, but did not join us because they feared the interruption would silence her again. They stood off in the distance and watched the episode with quiet amazement. Now they realized the elderly lady needed a friend unlike any she could find in the hospital, or in the home where she now resided.

Before we left that day, the daughter and the doctor were making plans to have someone visit every week and bring a dog, all because an elegant black poodle with a velvet tongue and soft brown eyes had done what no one else had been able to do. For awhile the dog had changed the old lady's heart rate, increased her blood flow and drawn back the curtain of silence to let her memories of years gone by rush through to fall on the ears of those who would listen. For a few minutes that sunny afternoon, the old lady communicated and participated. She was an active part of today rather than the faded memory of a day gone by. She was alive!

Today, twentieth-century scientists and doctors are realizing the value and effect of that intangible emotion known as love. Although no one can describe it, no medical books define it, no scientist can measure it and no doctor can hear it with a stethoscope, love is an essential ingredient in giving meaning to the quality of life. As powerful as the essence of love is to life, it is even more influential to death and there have been studies done within the last ten years to document that fact.

Back in 1948 a now famous medical study was begun in Framingham, Massachusetts, to determine the factors contributing to the deaths of people who died of heart disease. High serum cholesterol levels in the blood, smoking, obesity and several other factors were all suspect at the time. It was hoped that comparing the habits of those dying of heart disease in Framingham against those who died of other causes would accurately substantiate the contributing factors of deaths due to heart disease.

The study included more than five thousand people in that quiet, seemingly stable, little New England town where life is fairly constant and stress is not a major factor in those lives. People there work, play and pretty much conduct their lives in a routine sort of way. Participants of the study were checked every two years, and when they died the causes of their deaths were determined by autopsy and the facts of the deaths were carefully fed into computers.

Now, more than thirty years later, we know for certain that blood pressure, serum cholesterol, smoking and many other factors do in fact influence coronary heart disease. But what the study did not take into account was how many deaths in the Framingham project were premature and, of those, how many were influenced by the lack of human and/or animal companionship and love.

Dr. James Lynch, who participated in the Framingham study and wrote about it in a book titled *The Broken Heart* (Basic Books), has participated in other studies to find the answers to these and other questions related to premature deaths. At the University of Maryland School of Medicine where he is a Professor of Psychology, Dr. Lynch has studied hundreds of people in both the University Hospital's coronary care unit and the shock-trauma unit.

He has witnessed the deaths of people, young and old, who have died despite the fact that they were making good clinical recovery from heart attacks and accidents. In more than a few cases he has observed deaths that could only be caused by broken hearts. A person dies shortly after a spouse succumbs. A young woman dies shortly after her twin dies. An old man dies without cause and later it is learned he was alone in the world, without even a close friend.

Additional studies by Lynch and many other researchers show that the rate of premature deaths due to coronary disease is significant. For example, the premature death rate of nonmarried white males between the ages of 25 and 34 in the

United States is more than two-and-one-half times greater than that of married white males in the same age category.

The statistics for females isn't much better. Additionally, researchers have learned that all nonmarried people at all ages have higher death rates than comparable married individuals. The fact that single, divorced and widowed individuals die earlier than those who are married says a lot for togetherness.

All this data and much more seem to point very clearly to the idea that mankind would be wise to pay at least as much attention to the shape of this social status as he does to the shape of his body! Despite the fact that people today spend millions of dollars a year on sports equipment, jogging gear and exercise apparatus, modern man does not yet fully appreciate the power of love and companionship. Not only are they factors in keeping mankind well and happy, it appears now that love and companionship can help us live longer.

In a study with Dr. Aaron Katcher, Associate Professor of Psychiatry at the University of Pennsylvania, and Dr. Erika Friedman, Professor of Psychology at the University of Maryland Medical School, Lynch made another fascinating, related discovery. The team found that one year after heart attacks, 11 out of 39 patients who did not own pets died of a second heart attack whereas only 3 out of 53 patients who did own pets had succumbed.

Although the two groups represented a cross section of society, the only common factor among the group members was their ownership or lack of ownership of pets. It appears certain, from these and other studies, that the body's cardiovascular system is in fact more than slightly affected by love and companionship or the absence of it.

Since love and companionship are proving to be linked to longevity, then, ideally, premature deaths from heart disease could be reduced in number if only the people in question could find the right person with whom to share their lives. This, however, is often impossible for a variety of reasons, not the least of which is the technological style of life in this century and the fact that there are so many people in the world whose "ideal person" will never be found.

Our lifestyle is one of isolation in itself. Witness the fact that many people who live in large cities never get to know their own neighbors because each person is so wrapped up in his or her own activities and life there is no time or interest in developing friendships. And so, millions of people live and die alone and lonely.

In 1978 Dr. Katcher began a study to determine the relationship between human blood pressure and pets. In the experiment a group of people had their blood pressure recorded under three different conditions. First, they were in a room alone. Next, while they were reading to another person. And finally, while they were talking to and stroking a dog. The findings were startling. In a majority of cases, the blood pressure readings dropped significantly when the subjects were interacting with the dog!

Dogs, it appears, can do infinitely more than provide man with a feeling of security around the home, assist him in the sport of hunting and serve as a helper on the farm. They can hold back the creeping fog that tries so relentlessly to blur aging minds. They can tear down the invisible barriers of loneliness that surround the old and the sick. They can create a feeling of being needed for those who have all but given up the struggle to survive.

Because of researchers like Lynch, Katcher and Friedman, the old, the sick, the weak and the lonely are in fact experiencing a rejuvenating breath of freshness in their lives. In short, the researchers are learning that people no longer need to die of loneliness and broken hearts. Still others, singly and in groups, are organizing to see that they don't.

Individuals and organizations across America are dedicating their free time and talents to bringing new meaning to empty lives. By their actions they are saying, "We are here and we want to share with you. You are needed and appreciated just because you are you!" And dogs, because they are the most social of all animals, are improving the quality of those precious lives, whether they're destined to be on this earth for another day or a decade.

This isn't a thunderous, shotgun type of movement that is going to be obvious to the casual observer of life in general. Rather, it's going to be classically volcanic in its development, growing in muted rumbles, a small step here and another there, until a wave of involvement spreads its lava across most of the

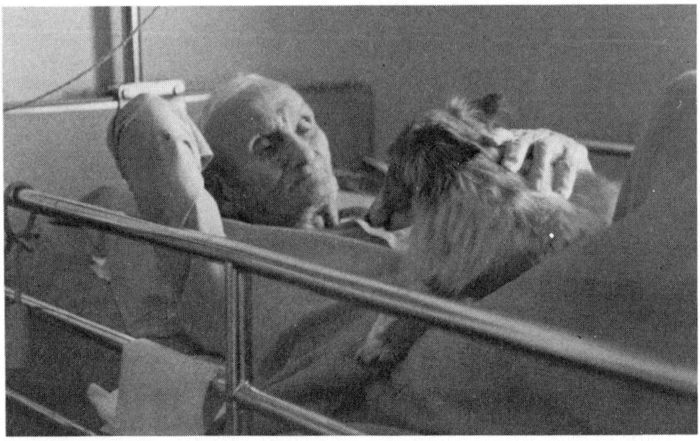

An aged man and a dog celebrate a moment together.
The Latham Foundation

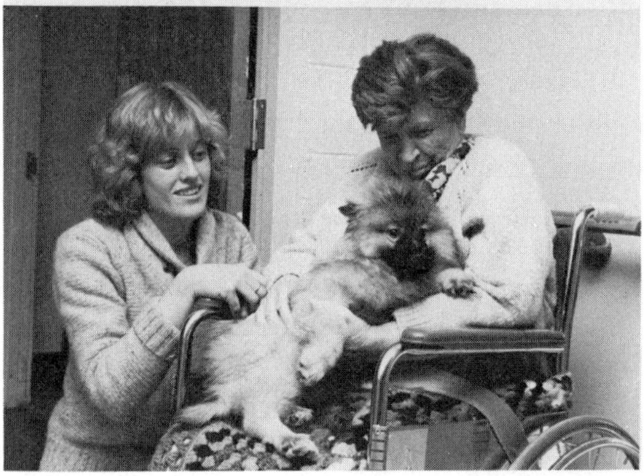

Words aren't necessary when a warm friend brings a smile to an elderly face. *The Latham Foundation*

A young man brings a fuzzy friend to visit an elderly lady. *The Latham Foundation*

countries of the civilized world. It's something like washing a batch of dirty clothes: you don't notice the clothes getting clean, you notice the water getting dirty.

For example, the American Veterinary Medical Association has formed a task force to explore the subject in its entirety. And state veterinary medical associations are jumping on the bandwagon, too. In California, for instance, the Contra Costa County Veterinary Medical Association has launched a "Pets by Rx" program to educate the general public about the therapeutic value of pets. In addition, "Pets by Rx" will assist nursing homes to obtain and maintain resident pets for the elderly.

In Maryland, at a place called the Chesapeake Bay Center for Environmental Studies, the Smithsonian Institute is studying the significance of the human/companion animal bond in a Family Learning Project. There a group of enthusiastic scientists and educators is attempting to strengthen the family unit, thereby producing stronger citizens and a more dynamic society.

Maryland is also the state in which approximately eighteen nursing homes are taking part in a pilot project begun in 1982 to introduce pets into their facilities. Diane C. Ritter, Recreational/Social Service Director and member of the advisory committee for developing criteria for allowing residential pets within health care facilities, says, "We're proud to be in the forefront of this relatively new and warming opportunity to improve the quality of life for the institutionalized elderly."

Many of America's major institutions of learning are recognizing and beginning to deal with the significance of the human/companion animal bond. The University of California at both Irvine and Davis, the Universities of Minnesota, Hawaii, and Pennsylvania, Penn State, Purdue, Cornell, Texas A & M, Colorado State and Michigan State are all getting involved. And the number grows weekly.

One of the leaders in the field of involvement in the human/companion animal bond is Dr. Leo K. Bustad, Dean of Washington State University's College of Veterinary Medicine. Dr. Bustad took the bull by the horns in 1974 when he began placing pets in nursing homes to alleviate the loneliness, the depression and the lack of interest in life itself that so many of the residents exhibited. Dr. Bustad has travelled to Melbourne, Australia; Bethel in Germany; Beitostole in Norway and St. Christopher's Hospice in England to study and promote the use of pets in homes for the aged. Using these experiences and many more he's had over the past sixty years, he has founded the People-Pet Partnership Program (PPP) at Washington State University in conjunction with the communities of Pullman, Washington, and nearby Moscow, Idaho. More than 150 veterinary students from Washington State University and citizens from surrounding cities volunteer their time and services to the program.

The PPP consists of three major areas of interest in the human/companion animal bond movement. The Public/Private School Partnership (PSP) serves to educate children about animal care. It teaches children how to choose a pet and focuses attention on responsible pet ownership.

The CAP, which stands for Companion Animal Partnership, explores the ways in which animals contribute to human life and facilitates visits of dogs and cats to nursing homes and homes for the aged. CAP also researches the therapeutic value of animals to noninstitutionalized individuals.

PETE is the Partnership in Equine Therapy and Education division of the People-Pet Partnership Program. Imagine a physically handicapped youngster sitting in the saddle of a great, noble horse. The feeling of being up so high and in control of oneself must be the most exhilarating experience of a lifetime. The physical benefits of riding, relaxation, muscle development and coordination are additional benefits that cannot be ignored. The whole experience can only lead to the development of self-esteem and a renewed interest in life itself.

In a pilot project, the PPP at Washington State has placed pets in two homes, the Paradise Villa Convalescent Center in Moscow, Idaho, and the Pullman Convalescent Center in Pullman, Washington. Under a grant from the Safeco Corporation, the programs are being observed and monitored to determine such factors as the ideal method of pet placement in facilities, ideal types of dogs for nursing and retirement homes, extent of resident-dog interaction necessary for optimum benefits, etc. When the project is completed and evaluated, a guideline book will be prepared and distributed to other facilities and organizations interested in pet-facilitated therapy.

Dr. Bustad, who in 1980 wrote a book titled *Animals, Aging, and the Aged* (University of Minnesota Press), is serving as an advisor to the project. Dr. Marie Zeglen, Director of Biomedical Communications at the College of Veterinary Medicine at Washington State, is the principal investigator on the project.

Linda M. Hines, MA, co-founder with Dr. Bustad and current Director of PPP, is also serving as a project advisor. She has recently completed writing a how-to book describing the PPP program, and is a full-time Director of Veterinary Public Relations and Development at Washington State.

Terry Ryan, of Pullman, Washington, will supervise the selection and training of the dogs for this project. A member of the National Association of Dog Obedience Instructors, Ms. Ryan has many years of experience training dogs and dog owners and is much involved in the study of canine behavior.

Dr. Ronnal L. Lee is serving as project consultant along with Susan Lundebjerg, BS, who will serve as participant observer as part of her masters thesis in veterinary science.

From this list one can see that this pilot project is no slack attempt at establishing the best possible methods of incorporating dogs into institutions specializing in the care of the infirm and elderly. With such a prestigious staff, canine and human medical personnel and administrative leaders around the world will be assured that the published results of the pet placement project have been carefully researched and precisely presented for optimal effectiveness. It becomes obvious, then, that pet-facilitated therapy is an idea on the threshold of the future and a reality in the early stages of its birth.

Across the country at Penn State University, Dr. Daniel Lago, Assistant Professor of Human Development, has developed a program for elderly people, most of whom live alone rather than in homes for the aged. In that program, Dr. Lago has placed 65 pets with aged people. His findings show that reclusive people with dogs become more socially active and healthier. In addition, dogs help disabled elderly people to rise above their disabilities and overcome depression.

Preliminary observations indicate a whole bevy of positive results arising out of the experience of owning and caring for pets. People have to get up in the morning to care for their pets. They have to prepare meals for their animals. They have to get out and buy food, exercise their dogs, communicate and interact with others as a direct result of pet ownership.

Dr. Lago tells about one lady who had a broken hip and was severely disabled. She was given a dog for protection and, one day, found herself running up the stairs to chase the dog. At that moment she discovered for the first time that she could navigate the stairs.

In Melbourne, Australia, Caulfield Geriatric Hospital has a Labrador Retreiver named Honey who has increased verbal communication, improved mobility and the feeling of well-being among the residents. Most importantly, perhaps, was the improvement in the relationship of the residents with the staff of Caulfield. Honey gave them something in common to share.

In London, England; Columbus, Ohio; Birmingham, Alabama; and dozens of other cities and towns around the world, people are beginning to recognize the newest value of dogs to humans. And, like the little lady that day at the garden party who spoke only to my Blondie, many troubled and lonely people find talking to a dog more rewarding than speaking to a hospital full of highly trained therapists.

For, as Dr. Bustad recently said, "Few are the people who do not benefit by association with animals. Companion animals offer us security, succor, esteem, understanding, forgiveness and abundant love. They make no judgments, and we can be ourselves around them. Furthermore, they need our help and make us feel important. Such a combination is hard to beat!"

Dogs That Aid the Handicapped

Crippled hands, so twisted and frail, they act like they can't tell the brain what they're going to do next. Watch them try to pick up a toothbrush, hold a coffee cup, open a drawer. It seems an eternity before they arrange themselves in the correct position to perform whatever simple task the brain commands.

Now watch these same weak, uncoordinated tools come to life and get control of themselves. Give them a leash and tell the owner to hook up his dog. As if by magic, they have purpose and respond, slowly, deliberately and with the strength of Goliath. For this is not just any dog's leash—this leash unites their owner with freedom, independence, love and self-esteem. This is life, baby! And the man who owns these hands was born anew the day this dog walked into his world.

. . . .

There are physically handicapped people in every country of the world. Some of them were born with their handicaps, others are accident victims. And, by virtue of the increasing world population, there will continue to be an increasing number of handicapped people.

No one knows for sure how many handicapped people there are in the world today, but ten years ago a famed rehabilitation specialist estimated there were 250,000 people in wheelchairs in the United States alone. If you consider the growth in world population in the last ten years and the rise in accidents due to the ever-growing mechanization of our society, you can see that the world's handicapped today must number over a million people. Until recently, most of these people have been institutionalized or confined to their homes.

However, we can no longer confine them to hospitals,

homes and institutions to live out their lives in social, economic and cultural isolation. They must be a contributing part of life's mainstream, living, loving, laughing and worrying with the rest of us. In fact, most of them want to do just that. So together we, both handicapped and nonhandicapped, must find ways to help these people lead rewarding, useful lives. Fortunately for mankind in general, a few far-sighted organizations and individuals, some handicapped, others not, have seriously considered the needs of the handicapped and realized that dogs can play a significant role in returning them to their places in society.

Notable among the nonprofit organizations actively engaged in providing specially trained dogs to help handicapped people develop independent skills are: Canine Companions for Independence in Santa Rosa, California, founded in 1975; Handi-Dogs, Inc., Tucson, Arizona, founded in 1974; and the Aid Dogs for the Handicapped Foundation in Oreland, Pennsylvania, founded in 1969. Some provide trained dogs for the handicapped. Others help the handicapped to train their own dogs. All have developed a variety of training methods necessary to train each dog to meet its owner's unique needs.

Both Canine Companions for Independence and Aid Dogs obtain puppies, place them in puppy-rearing foster homes until the dogs are about eighteen months of age, supervise their basic obedience training and general socialization and, finally, place them with the handicapped where they begin custom training for their life's work with the owner. Only Handi-Dogs takes handicapped people who have dogs of their own and trains the dogs and people to work together. In this case, no puppy rearing facilities are necessary since the dogs that come to them for training are already in their permanent homes.

Canine Companions, founded by Bonnie Bergin, offers three separate types of dogs: signal dogs, social dogs and service dogs. Each type is designed to meet the specific needs of the people with whom they will live and eventually work.

Signal dogs are trained to assist the hearing impaired. They alert the deaf owner to bells and sirens ringing, babies crying, alarms sounding and many other noises in the owners' environment that would ordinarily be missed by the deaf.

Social dogs offer love and companionship to lonely elders

living in homes for the aged and other institutions. The nonjudgmental affection offered by social dogs to autistic children and severely retarded young people often serves to break the barriers of social isolation that surrounds these patients. Medical and health care workers frequently observe dramatic improvements in the patient's abilities to interact with other humans following exposure to social dogs. Although there is a growing number of institutions that have dogs in residence, most arrange for dogs to visit on a regular basis.

Service dogs are trained to help the handicapped with daily tasks as simple as picking up dropped items and proceeding upwards to such difficult behaviors as opening elevator doors and turning light switches on and off. Each service dog is custom trained and actually spends much of its life learning new behaviors as its owner's needs change and grow. A dog, for example, that begins life with a person who is totally confined to a wheelchair may, in time, find himself having to carry crutches to his owner as the patient's condition improves and he becomes more ambulatory. A wheelchair user may begin life after an accident in the home of a relative. There the dog's use is limited to times when the patient is home alone or when he and the dog go outside together. However, as the person gains confidence in his own abilities and adjusts to his handicap, he may move into a house or apartment of his own. Then the dog will be required to participate much more intensely in daily activities and, in addition, develop a mild sense of protectiveness. Wherever he lives and regardless of the degree of involvement with its handicapped owner, the service dog's biggest contribution to its owner remains its ability to offer unequivocal love and companionship. Whatever its category of service, Canine Companions for Independence has seen many of its graduates broaden their horizons by going to college, getting jobs and beginning to function in society as a result of their service dogs.

Aid Dogs is limited to assisting the severely physically handicapped. Founder and President Starr Hayes is the guiding force behind the dramatic list of achievements accomplished by the organization. It has provided, free of charge, trained dogs to over a dozen handicapped people, most of whom are paraplegics or quadraplegics. They train Golden Retrievers exclusively, all of which are spayed bitches.

Hayes begins looking for a potential owner when each puppy is approximately eight months old. At first, the dog meets the prospective new owner when the handicapped person observes the dog in an obedience class situation, or when the dog is brought to the handicapped person's home to visit. The meetings are short, friendly and very rewarding for both pup and potential owner. As the bond begins to develop, the pup's training is geared to the potential new owner's needs.

Once the dog moves into its new home, Hayes continues to work with the team during the period of custom training. In addition, Hayes further cements the bond by presenting the new owner with a puppy scrapbook, detailing the first year of the dog's life so that he feels a part of his dog's puppyhood. As with all similar organizations, Aid Dogs keeps in touch with its graduates and offers additional training and problem solving as the needs arise.

Perhaps the organization that has, to date, produced the most assistance dogs for the physically handicapped is Handi-Dogs, Inc., Tucson, Arizona. Founded in 1974 by Alamo Reaves, a wheelchair user herself, the organization began with a class of nine handicapped dog owners, each of whom trained their own dog in basic obedience and specialized behaviors. Class size has grown over the years to the present-day enrollment of thirty-five students with two sessions per year. Many of the students, although handicapped, are ambulatory.

Each student trains his or her own dog assisted by volunteers. Each lesson is customized to the limitations of the student. Pure-breds and mixed breeds are eligible for training providing they have short or easy-care coats, good temperaments and are healthy and housebroken.

Handi-Dogs trains dogs for the deaf as well as the disabled, and has a group of volunteers who take dogs to visit nursing homes and day care centers.

There are growing numbers of individuals who are spending more and more of their time and talents in training dogs to serve their handicapped owners. The dogs, in turn, are learning to perform an almost unbelievable variety of tasks destined to improve the quality of life for their owners.

In Newport Beach, California, a young woman, Sue Myles, has established a school called Able Dogs where handicapped

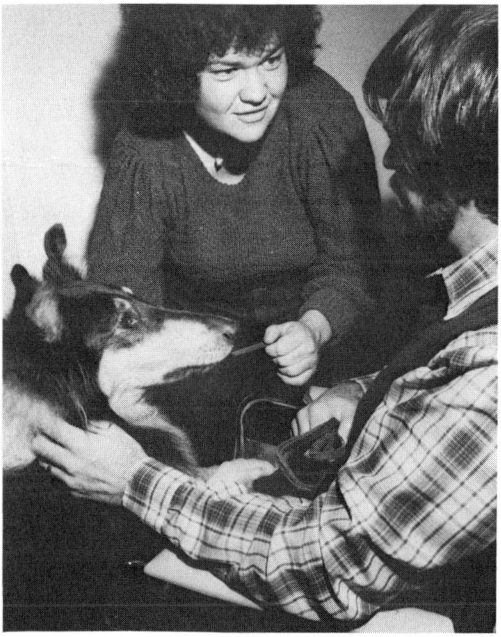

Sue Myles introduces Katy, the Collie, to a handicapped handler. Notice the man's hand immediately reaches out to touch the dog.
Rosenfeld

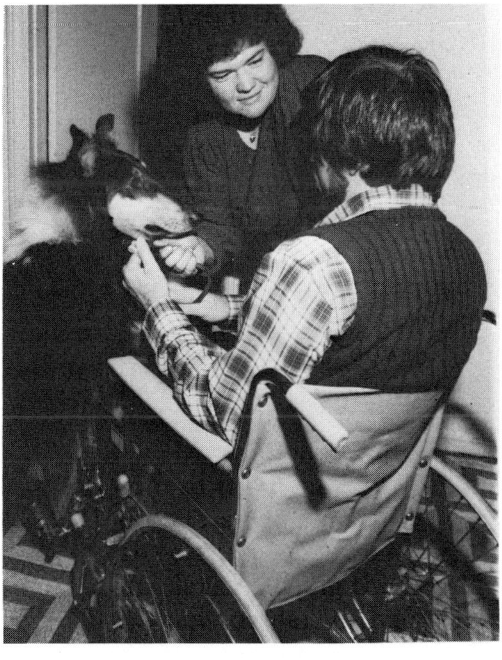

Sue Myles shows the handicapped handler how to teach Katy to sit up, placing her paws on his lap.
Rosenfeld

dog owners train their dogs to assist them. Myles has also been extremely successful in training handicapped children to train their own dogs.

Through training their dogs, the children have learned responsibility and decision making, something they rarely get to learn elsewhere. They are more active, more independent and more productive in their chosen fields of interest because of their involvement with training dogs as partners. But the most striking achievement of all for the children is the confidence they develop in themselves. A dog never complains when one is wrong or slow or clumsy; he just keeps on loving.

Terry Ryan, in Pullman, Washington, does just about the same thing as Myles. She takes handicapped people and dogs that nobody wants and teaches them all to live and work together to make both human and canine lives more meaningful. A multiple sclerosis victim and a man who suffered brain damage in an auto accident were just two of her many students within the recent past.

Sue Myles and Terry Ryan are not alone. There are many individual dog trainers and instructors across the country who are helping people help themselves and using dogs to do it. In many basic dog training classes, one can find handicapped people training their own dogs. Of course, we're not talking here about the severely handicapped. Rather, we're referring to people such as an arthritis victim who can't bend over to pick up objects from the floor, a person who has a pacemaker or a mastectomy patient whose arm and shoulder are weakened and can't hold packages. These are the people for whom dogs can be trained to make their lives easier, more pleasant, broader and more rewarding. To those who have lost a measure of independence because of illness or accident, having a dog as a helping partner makes life worth living once again.

In many states dogs that aid the handicapped can be certified by a board of examiners and allowed to accompany their owners into restaurants, on public transportation and in other places where pets are not normally allowed. The certification gives them the same privileges as guide dogs for the blind.

There are a few organizations working on a national level toward getting certification in all states. Although their number is small now, they are being joined by others as the pet-people-partnership program receives more recognition and appreciation.

One of the biggest changes already taking place with regard to dogs and other pets that aid the handicapped is in public housing. Until recently, landlords could prohibit tenants from owning pets. Now, however, many states are passing laws, most of which were tested in court, that permit people to own pets when it is determined that the pets in question are in some way beneficial to the health and well-being of the tenant.

In an editorial in *The Latham Letter,* the newsletter of the Latham Foundation, a world renowned organization dedicated to the promotion of respect for all life through education, the group's President, Hugh H. Tebault, writes of the significance of the human/companion animal bond:

"An understanding of the significance of the human/companion animal bond can hold great value for every one of us. For the human health professional, prescription of a companion animal can be an effective tool in meeting psychiatric, physical or social problems. For the veterinarian such prescriptions can bring about an enhanced professional image and great satisfaction as the scope of his art is enlarged through an understanding of the bond's importance to his human clients. Humane educators who through the years have told us to be kind to animals now can tell us why. For the average person concerned with the resolution of physical, mental or emotional problems, his own, or those of his family or friends, a knowledge of the value of the human/companion animal bond can be truly meaningful. Commercial organizations, pet food, veterinary pharmaceutical and pet supply manufacturers and distributors have long been criticized for their preoccupation with pets rather than humans—why are we spending money on pets when children are starving? For them the 'bond' can be the basis for building a new corporate character, a fine public image for producing products which figure significantly in enhancing the basic well-being not only of companion animals, but of their owners.

"Up to now the emphasis of those professionals who are prescribing animals to help meet human problems has mostly been as therapy for people with special problems. Considering the unprecedented stress which 'normal people' experience in today's pressured urban society, we would like also to see broader acceptance of the value of companion animals for everyone.

"In our opinion, failure to recognize, study and employ the benefits of the human/companion animal bond as a highly significant, available, cost-effective resource is to ignore a magnificent scientific breakthrough and to deny society a phenomenal new resource."

As we have seen modern medicine and scientific research have proven that pets are more than mere entertainment for most people. And this kind of documentation is hard to argue with in a court of law.

Despite the threat of nuclear devastation and international conflicts that plague us daily (or maybe because of it!), people all over the world are helping people live better lives by teaching canines of every size and description to do things we never dreamed they could do just a few short years ago. And dogs, as they have for thousands of years, are proving that prehistoric man did indeed make a wise decision to domesticate the ancestors of the wild dog.

Keith Wilbur and Larry Clott

This is the story of two men, one in Oreland, Pennsylvania, the other in Moscow, Idaho. Both are married, have no children and each owns a dog. Their dogs are very special dogs, but then the men are very special, too. Both are quadraplegics confined to wheelchairs. But the most common feature the two possess is their indomitable will to be independent and demonstrate, through their own accomplishments, that one need not stop living when faced with adversity.

In 1976 Keith Wilbur was a college student at Lutheran Theological Seminary at Philadelphia, Pennsylvania. He was tall and thin, newly married to a pretty blond wisp of a girl named Nancy and very involved in one of the busiest, most exciting periods of his life. Then one day, as he was sleeping, he suffered a massive stroke.

Following his initial hospitalization, Keith spent six months in the Moss Rehabilitation Center in Philadelphia where he learned how to live from a wheelchair. By the time he was ready to leave, it was obvious that his entire left side was affected and his speech and sight were permanently and severely impaired.

With the determination of youth, Keith returned home to his bride and resolved to pick up the pieces of his life where he'd left off. He'd master the art of self-care, help Nancy around the house, finish his education and, through some type of therapeutic work, inspire other handicapped people to grab onto the tail of life and live it. He had no intention of giving up. Instead, he would show others how to fight back, too.

Shortly after he returned home, Keith met Mandy. Mandy is a Golden Retriever and an Aid Dog for the Handicapped. He first saw her while she was participating in an obedience class with her foster owner. The meeting was short, friendly and a very positive experience for them both.

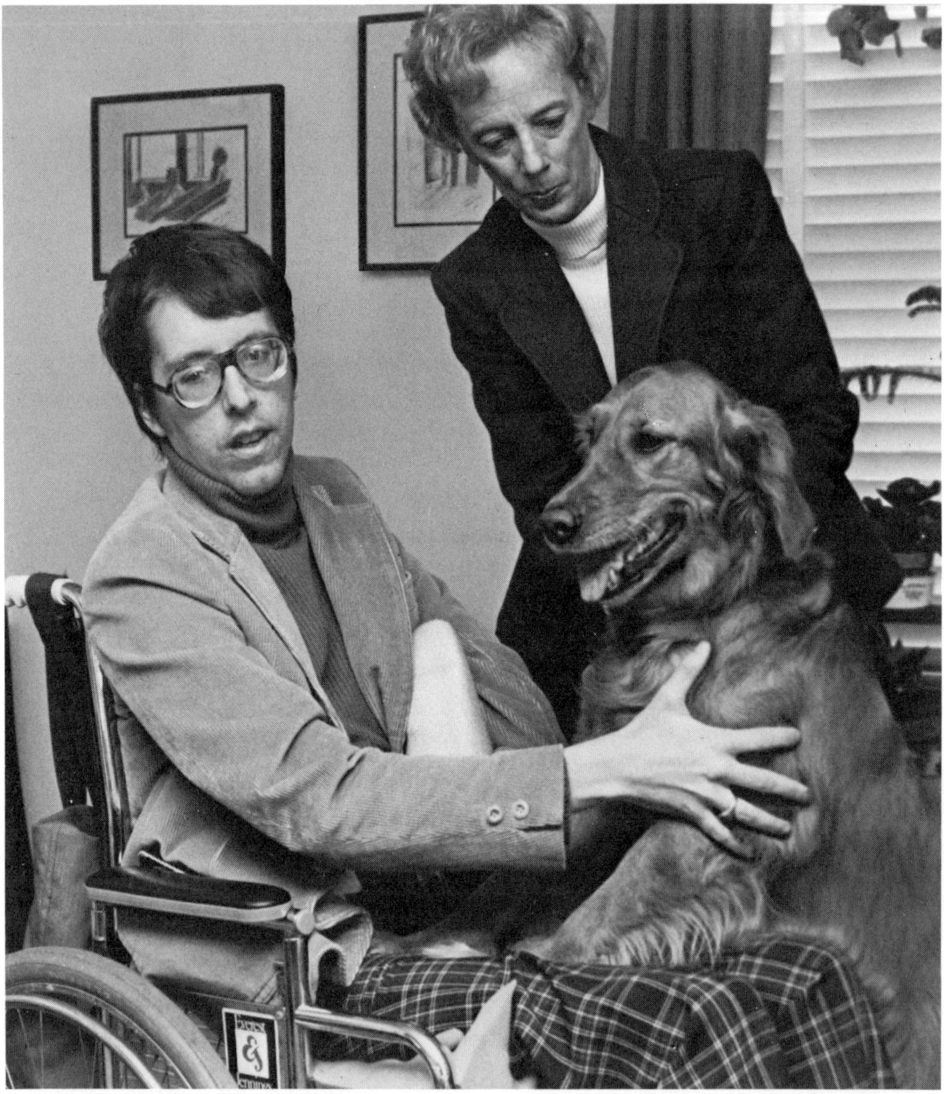

Keith Wilbur and Aid Dogs for the Handicapped Foundation President Starr Hayes admire Golden Retriever Mandy. *Ken Parlini*

As the weeks wore on, Keith got to know Mandy well as he observed her each week in her class. By the time the course was completed, Mandy and Keith had begun establishing the bond that would carry them through a lifetime together.

In obedience class, Mandy learned the basic behaviors of being gentle and obedient. She also learned to pick up objects from the floor and carry items from one place to another. Upon graduation, she left her foster home to become Keith's full-time partner.

In her new home, Mandy began her advanced training under the tutelage of Starr Hayes from the Aid Dogs for the Handicapped Foundation. Her lessons were designed to fill Keith Wilbur's unique needs and the lifestyle she'd be living.

First, she had to learn to understand Keith's commands, which he gives in a monotone caused by his speech impairment. A tape recording of Hayes' voice giving a command coupled with Keith's in-person command helped her transfer from the clearly spoken word to the guttural sounds of a monotone.

Once she began to understand Wilbur, she learned to bring in the mail, retrieve whatever Wilbur needed when asked to do so, open doors and act as guardian and companion twenty-four hours a day.

In short, she gave Keith Wilbur independence and freedom. And he gave Mandy a new meaning and purpose to her life. Together, they became a team.

Before Mandy came, Keith could not be left alone. Now, however, Nancy has returned to her job at a large pharmaceutical company nearby while Keith keeps the home fires burning. From his wheelchair, he makes his own lunch, vacuums and keeps the house tidy, answers the telephone, takes physical therapy from a visiting nurse three days a week and cares for Mandy and his own personal needs, all with Mandy's help.

Now, six years later, the hurricane of disaster has passed the Wilbur household. In its path stands a man and a woman with a bushy-tailed Golden Retriever, each caught up in their activities of today and their plans for the future.

In 1981 the Wilburs became foster owners, for the Aid Dog Foundation, of another Golden Retriever named Chris. Nancy taught her basic obedience and retrieving. Keith and Mandy taught her house manners, the art of gentleness and how to do many of the jobs she'd be performing for her future owner, a young quadraplegic man in South Carolina. When Chris was twenty months old, she went to live with her new owner and begin her life of service.

Meanwhile, Nancy became so caught up with the fascination of teaching dogs, she volunteered her services to the Aid Dog Foundation and is now assistant to its President and Chief Trainer, Starr Hayes. Several nights a week, she leaves Keith and Mandy at home and goes to the local YMCA to teach dog obedience to other dogs and their owners.

Keith, on the other hand, went back to his books to finish what he had begun six years ago. Using tape cassettes to compensate for his poor eyesight, he has now earned a master's degree in religious art. Eventually, he plans to take speech therapy to regain some of the vocal ability he lost.

The future? It looks exciting for the Wilbur family. Nancy has a new Golden Retriever puppy, named Kelly, to train and keep. She'll continue working with the Aid Dog Foundation in whatever capacity she's needed. Keith and Mandy will help in Kelly's rearing, and teach her to help in many ways around the house.

As for Keith, he intends to devote his time and energy to overcoming his disabilities and offering support and encouragement to others with similar problems. He and Mandy will go to hospitals and rehabilitation centers to demonstrate that life need not end when one loses physical skills.

When asked what he thinks of the idea of using dogs to aid the handicapped, Keith Wilbur said, "The use of aid dogs is dynamic in helping wheelchair users. Instead of looking at dogs solely as pets, we must realize dogs can be an outgrowth of the person himself. The relationship and the potential to be an extension of the individual is exciting and I'll use my experience to help teach others."

The other half of the story comes from three thousand miles away in Moscow, Idaho. There, a young man goes to work, lives a full life and keeps busy all because he has a dog named Kuna to help him.

The story goes something like this: A 1969 automobile accident left Larry Clott a quadraplegic confined to a

Mandy fetches brace for her owner, Keith Wilbur. *Ken Parlini*

Mandy fetches the all-important transfer board for her owner, Keith Wilbur. *Ken Parlini*

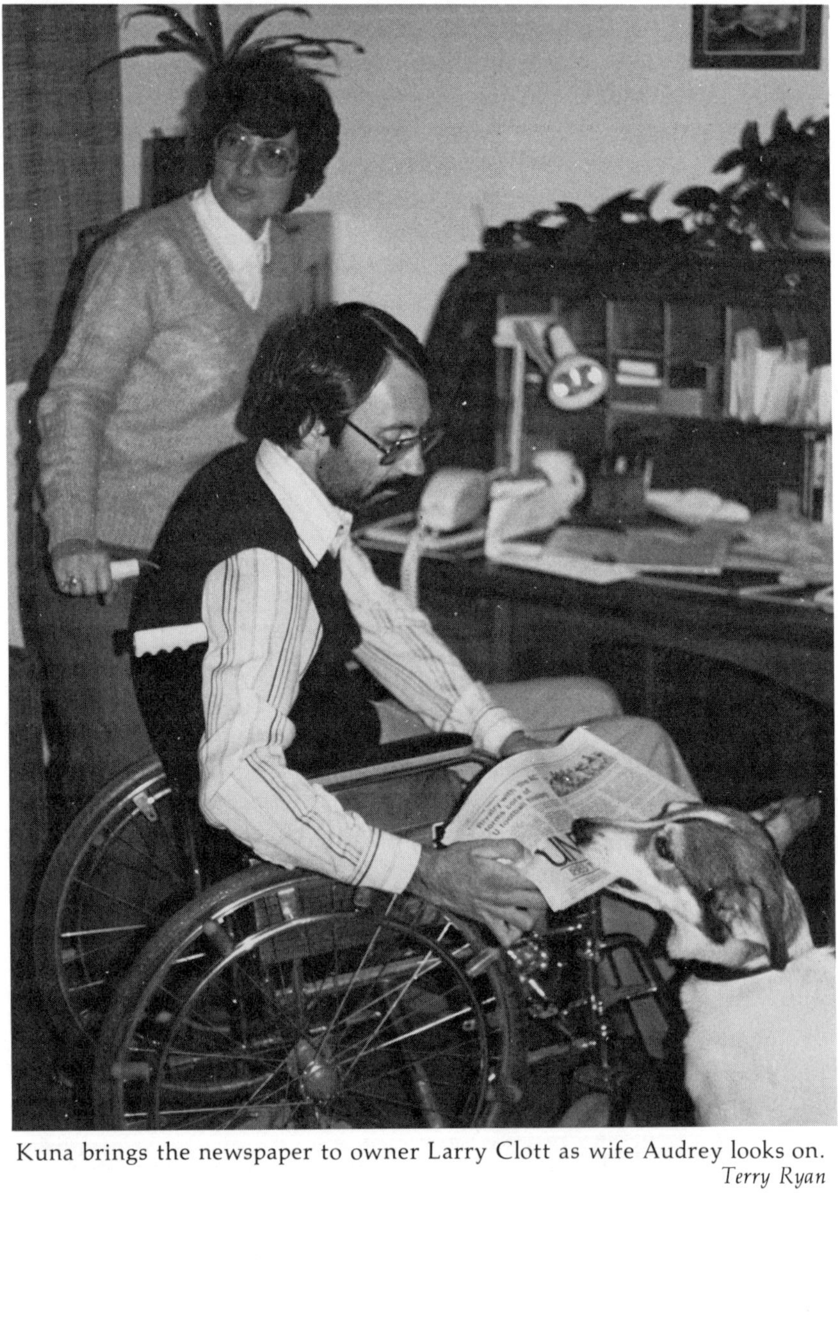

Kuna brings the newspaper to owner Larry Clott as wife Audrey looks on.
Terry Ryan

wheelchair. After the usual rounds of hospitalization and rehabilitation, Larry continued to work and function totally dependent on his wife, Audrey, for help. Then, in early 1981, Larry and Audrey adopted a mixed breed dog, half German Shepherd Dog and half Siberian Husky, by the name of Kuna. She had originally been adopted from the Spokane Humane Society, but when she was about a year old her owners decided they couldn't keep her so the Clotts became her second owners.

At first, the Clotts spent hours socializing Kuna so she could overcome her shyness. In addition, they worked on getting control of her hyperactive behavior. Eventually, Kuna calmed down and was able to learn new things. Then there were all her bad habits that had to be corrected, but the Clotts persevered and Kuna finally began to respond to the Clotts' gentle understanding and their lifestyle.

When Kuna was two years old, Larry Clott enrolled in an obedience class under the tutelage of a lady named Terry Ryan, who has had a great deal of experience teaching handicapped handlers and dogs. Kuna needed a lot of work because she was shy, overactive and prone to misbehaving. Clott and Ryan, however, vowed to persist with Kuna's training.

Together, they taught Kuna how to be gentle, obey commands and retrieve. The dog learned how to walk calmly on the right side of Larry's wheelchair, come when called and pick up anything that he might drop.

Since Larry's entire body and hands were affected by the paralysis in his spine, he lost most of the dexterity in his hands and is prone to dropping things. Kuna has now become an extra hand to her owner. She is also helpful in turning light switches on and off, and alerts him to danger when they're away from home together—and they're away frequently.

Five days a week, Kuna accompanies Larry Clott to his job as a Program Counselor at Stepping Stones, Inc., a firm that works with handicapped people in Moscow, Idaho. Once they arrive at Larry's desk, Kuna lays quietly beside her master, waiting to be asked to do something for him.

When Larry goes shopping, Kuna goes too, and the shopkeepers have become accustomed to seeing the two as they make their rounds together. The most important contribution Kuna makes to Larry's life, however, is the companionship she provides. As time goes on, she will continue to learn new ways to help him such as pushing elevator buttons and locating items by name for him.

"I didn't realize how much Kuna could learn," says Larry Clott. "I see now that service dogs can be invaluable to the handicapped."

Although Kuna did not come to the Clotts through the channels of an organization such as the Aid Dog for the Handicapped Foundation, he recommends that anyone interested in obtaining a service dog do so by contacting an organization near their home. It was a long, difficult process to rehabilitate Kuna and an organization would choose and train the dog specifically for its handicapped owner, thereby saving months of work and possible failure in the end.

Instructor Terry Ryan says of Larry and Kuna, "I wasn't in on the selection of Kuna, but she has progressed remarkably since Larry and Audrey began training her. I think Larry would agree with me when I say that a person should go to an organization or individual who has a background in training service dogs to get just the right dog for the job."

Kuna, on the other hand, proves to both Ryan and Clott almost daily how intelligent and willing to work she really is. Not only does she help Larry in a myriad of chores at home and in his office, she also serves as the mascot for the children's baseball team he coaches. In addition, Kuna has learned to fetch both Audrey and Cecile, Larry's secretary, by name. "This eliminates the fear of me having an accident and not having someone know about it," says Larry.

In his spare time, Larry Clott listens to music, watches spectator sports and spends a great deal of time with Kuna. "My life has changed drastically since I got Kuna. She gives me a certain sense of freedom. And it's a wonderful feeling."

That feeling is precisely what Clott is trying to impart to the many handicapped people with whom he comes into contact. Through his involvement with his work, his friends, his baseball team, he is proving that life for the disabled need not stop. He urges them to get involved, become familiar with life at its fullest and take advantage of the world around them.

And if a dog can help a person overcome some difficulties, "Go to it!," he says. He should know. With Kuna's help, he's overcome more than most.

Eyes at the End of the Leash

I see the children playing on the sidewalk ahead of me. The toddler riding his tricycle in the driveway. The willow branch hanging over the path in the park.

I regard the uncovered manhole and skirt around it. I observe the traffic crossing my path and stop. I see the marble steps of the museum. The garden gate and the car parked in front of my house.

I see them all, yet I see none of them for I am blind. My eyes see only darkness. Yet, through my guide dog, I see all the world and I am free.

. . . .

Early in mankind's history, blind people were treated as if they were totally useless, even to themselves. They were fed and cared for by loved ones and left to vegetate their lives away.

As time evolved, someone invented "caning" for the blind. A cane is a long, thin stick used to probe the ground ahead of the user to determine obstacles in his way.

By the year 100 B.C. a blind man found he could rely on his dog to guide him. Wall paintings in Pompeii depicted a dog guiding a blind person. In the sixth century, a saint used one to guide him through his ministries. By the thirteenth century, written reference to dogs guiding the blind were recorded in both China and Europe. Even Rembrandt and Gainsborough painted them.

Mankind in general was waiting for a spirited young man by the name of Morris Frank and a dedicated lady named Dorothy Eustis to organize and lead the guide dog concept in America. The year was 1929.

Frank had just returned from Mt. Pelerin, Switzerland,

By the time he is matched with a blind student, a Seeing Eye dog will go FORWARD only when his owner commands him to do so, and then, only if it is safe to cross. *E. James Pitrone*

with his first guide dog, a German Shepherd Dog he named Buddy. The dog had been trained at Fortunate Fields and was the first guide dog to be trained there for the purpose of guiding blind people.

Fortunate Fields was founded in 1923 by Dorothy Eustis, a wealthy Philadelphian. Her goal was to breed and train German Shepherd Dogs with an emphasis on producing dogs of superior working ability.

The dogs from Fortunate Fields served European armies and police departments. They were trained as messenger dogs for a communications unit of the Swiss Army. They laid communications wire, served as patrols in penitentiaries and performed all sorts of jobs requiring intelligence, independence and the ability to make decisions on their own.

The connection between Dorothy Eustis and the guide dog program in the United States is explained by Catherine W. Swan, Assistant Director of Development and Public Information at The Seeing Eye in Morristown, New Jersey. She recounts the chain of events preceding the actual formation of the first guide dog school in this country.

"Dorothy Eustis had associated herself with a man named Jack Humphrey, who was interested in breeding and training dogs. He was with Mrs. Eustis in Switzerland and was responsible for training the dogs at Fortunate Fields. The training itself was actually done as an adjunct to the breeding program, in a sense to prove out the breeding, or show that it was successful."

As Mrs. Eustis's success grew, she wrote an article about dogs guiding German war veterans. It was published in the *Saturday Evening Post* in the United States, and this article led Morris Frank to Fortunate Fields.

He wrote her requesting she train a dog to guide him just as the dogs of Germany guided the blind veterans about whom she'd written. She wrote back and invited him to come to Fortunate Fields where she presented him with Buddy.

Frank and Buddy returned to the United States in 1929. Frank was so impressed with his new companion and the freedom that Buddy afforded him, he wanted to help establish a school in his hometown of Nashville, Tennessee.

"The Seeing Eye," says Ms. Swan, "was founded in Nash-

Each dog is tested for safety in traffic with the instructor under blindfold.
E. James Pitrone

Students learn to tuck their Seeing Eye dogs under small tables while dining at The Seeing Eye.
E. James Pitrone

ville by Mrs. Eustis. She sent Jack Humphrey to the school to initiate the training program. On the way to Nashville, Humphrey stopped to visit a friend, Willi Ebeling from Lake Openaka, New Jersey. Ebeling, a wealthy, retired businessman, bred working-type German Shepherd Dogs.

"Ebeling became so interested in The Seeing Eye project, he decided to go to Nashville with Humphrey. However, problems with the dogs caused by the extreme heat of the South plagued Frank and Ebeling.

"Eventually the men moved The Seeing Eye school to Ebeling's kennels in Dover, New Jersey. The actual training took place in Morristown, just as it does today. The school, which was finally established in Whippany, New Jersey, was moved to our present facility in Morris Township in 1965.

About the time that Frank, Ebeling and Humphrey were establishing the school, Mrs. Eustis was planning to establish a school for guide dog instructors. It would be a school where the apprentice instructors would spend a month with their eyes blindfolded so they might better understand what being blind felt like. Ultimately, she opened the school at her home in Mt. Pelerin.

From that early beginning, The Seeing Eye became a leader in the guide dog field. Today there are at least nine guide dog schools in the United States alone. The German Shepherd Dogs have been joined by Labrador and Golden Retrievers, and an occasional mix.

The training of a guide dog begins when he is a puppy. He is given some basic obedience work in a foster home where he is raised by a family until he is approximately twelve months old. Once he reaches adulthood, he is returned to the school. There he begins to build a rapport with his handler, the instructor. He is taught to sit, down, stay and walk slightly ahead of the handler in preparation for the day when he will guide a blind master.

More sophisticated training occurs when the dog is taught to lead the handler around obstacles, away from low-hanging objects such as tree branches, stop at curbs before crossing streets and board buses and trains. Finally, customized training involves teaching the dog whatever he needs to know to guide his new owner in that particular person's lifestyle.

Once the dog has completed his training, he is introduced to his new owner with whom he has been carefully paired. In most guide dog schools, the blind owner lives and trains at the school for up to four weeks before he and his dog graduate.

Back home, the blind person can resume a normal life with activities such as full-time employment, socializing and pursuing whatever interest he chooses. He quickly adjusts to the idea that his guide dog will always be with him.

As the dog and blind owner build a close relationship with each other, the dog usually assumes more responsibility for the welfare of his owner. The dog learns to "read" the body language of his master to better understand his commands and behavior.

Occasionally, a guide dog must disobey a command. If, for example, a blind person commands his dog to "forward" and the dog realizes impending danger in that action, the dog must refuse the command. In so doing, guide dogs have saved the lives of many blind owners.

A relationship of this intensity reaches far above the level of the ordinary man/dog kinship. Indeed, it frequently evokes the development of certain characteristics and behaviors of the blind that, in turn, serves to improve the quality of life.

The guide dog is not just a trained animal to be used when a blind person wishes to go from one place to another. The guide dog is a companion to its master. He is warm and loving, and offers unequivocal devotion without passing judgment.

Furthermore, he requires care and attention. The owner must maintain a regular schedule of care and exercise for the dog that helps to build muscles and improve physical coordination in both owner and dog.

Getting out regularly also creates opportunities for social contacts for the master. Those contacts frequently broaden the blind person's world and bring him personal freedom, a quality which is so necessary for emotional actualization.

In short, a guide dog acts as a link between the blind master and the seeing world. Modern technology has recently produced some phenomenal electronic equipment to aid the blind in many areas of life, but the guide dog will always remain the blind person's eyes at the end of the leash.

Debbie and Dutchess

Debbie Hoster was born with cerebral palsy and retinitis pigmentosa. Today, at age twenty-three, she is legally blind, walks with an erratic gait and has a speech impediment that makes her stutter at the slightest hint of anxiety. Despite all these problems, Debbie is a go-get-it, fun-to-be-with young woman who is busy making the world a better place to live in.

As a teenager, Debbie attended a regular high school in her home town of Burlington, New Jersey, where she excelled in her scholastic work. Later, she went to the Newtown School for the Blind in Pennsylvania to study office skills and self-maintenance proficiency.

When Debbie was a junior in high school, she begged her parents for a Doberman Pinscher puppy. Finally, unable to resist her pleas any more, they purchased a female puppy that Debbie promptly named Dutchess. It wasn't long before they enrolled in one of the obedience classes at Brandy Lane Farm Dog Training School in nearby Mount Holly, New Jersey.

While Dutchess was learning the ABC's of being an obedient, well-mannered dog, Debbie was blossoming as a unique young lady, full of spirit and good humor, with a whale-sized sense of determination both for herself and her dog. Debbie did things she's never done before. She learned to run, wobbly perhaps, but nonetheless run. She learned how to project her voice and stop stuttering when she spoke to Dutchess. She learned to "feel" the dog next to her instead of see her.

Most of all, the young girl with the ready smile made friends with other dog owners and began traveling to dog shows with them. For the first time in her life, she had to function independently of her parents. She learned she can do whatever she sets her mind to do. Most of all, she learned a

Handicapped owner Debbie Hoster and Dutchess, her Doberman Pinscher, on their way to training class. *Ken Parlini*

great deal about herself and that, in turn, gave her the self-confidence she needed to show Dutchess at American Kennel Club sanctioned obedience trials and earn a Companion Dog title for the dog.

She has since trained two other dogs and earned CD titles with them both. In 1982 she began showing still another dog, a Miniature Schnauzer named Crystal. Through it all, however, Dutchess has remained Debbie's constant companion, best friend and most supportive assistant.

As Debbie's rapport with Dutchess grew, they branched out to more sophisticated areas of training and developed a genuine working relationship together. Dutchess learned to be a back-packer. She and Debbie walked forest trails together, Dutchess carrying food and essentials for them both in a back-pack. An extremely intelligent Doberman, she learned to identify objects such as socks, a hat, a toy, her brush and Debbie's gloves by name. Today, Dutchess will retrieve whatever Debbie requests simply on verbal command.

Debbie's safety and security are also assured now because Dutchess has been trained to summon help whenever Debbie needs it. If Debbie should fall when they're out together and be unable to get up or, in some way, need help and be unable, due to her speech impairment, to call out for help, Dutchess will bring help to her mistress. The tall, black Dobe gently tugs at a coatsleeve, a jacket pocket or whatever she can sink her teeth into to get a person to follow her to Debbie. And she will not relent until that person responds by going to see Debbie.

For fun Debbie listens to popular and country western music, talking books and attends concerts whenever the opportunity arises. She has "seen" Frank Sinatra, Ronnie Milsap and Barry Manilow, all of whom rank high among her favorite musical artists.

Making latch hook rugs and teaching Dutchess tracking are her latest interests, and she spends time each day doing aerobic exercises to keep in shape for her other activities.

For Dutchess, fun has been learning to identify the primary colors, a behavior considered most difficult to teach dogs. She found it exciting and rather easy. She has also learned to identify and retrieve wooden letters so that, ultimately, she will be able to spell words with them. Through their training school,

Dutchess retrieves Debbie's hat. *Ken Parlini*

Dutchess convinces Debbie there is danger in her path and guides her around the construction material. *Ken Parlini*

Debbie and Dutchess give demonstrations at schools, homes for the aged and hospitals. They encourage others to get involved with a canine companion and show, by their demonstrations, how rewarding that involvement can be.

K-9 Capers, the exhibition team from Brandy Lane Farm, takes a lot of time from Debbie's days. Not only does she participate with Dutchess in all their shows, but Debbie serves as the most effective and efficient public relations manager the team has ever had. Despite her vocal handicap, she spends hours on the telephone arranging shows, making new dates and coordinating the team's affairs with institutions and organizations. And she does it all with that ever-present smile in her voice because she loves what she does.

"Music," she says, "is my hobby, but dogs are my life. I'd be lonely and helpless without Dutchess. With her I have things to do and places to go and people to enjoy. My life has meaning and every day she makes me want to get up and get out."

In the future, Debbie and Dutchess will continue to live, work and grow together toward an end that means assistance, independence and companionship to a bright young woman who otherwise would be confined to an easy chair and a record player. Dutchess is an extension of Debbie. And everyone who meets the pretty girl with the warm smile and the big dog with the regal bearing admires them both.

Dogs and Learning Disabled and Emotionally Disturbed Children

Picture this: Rene, a fourteen-year-old girl, moderately retarded, partially deaf as a result of spinal meningitis in early life, emotionally disturbed and reclusive because she has never been socialized or sent to school in her entire life. Now she is alone and even more reclusive and disturbed because of the death of her mother, the only person in the world to whom she responded.

Try this one on for size: A little boy, age nine, named Frank who is retarded, emotionally disturbed and suffers from psychotic behavior patterns that are socially unacceptable. Therapists cannot communicate with him in order to begin constructive treatment of his problems. Prognosis: Hopeless.

Now this: An autistic, mentally retarded girl, age six, has never spoken a word. Not one. No person, no therapy, no medication has ever managed to break her silence.

And finally: A mentally retarded boy, Robbie, whose disability was caused by RH blood factor incompatibility, is cared for at home by his parents. However, his retardation has caused him to withdraw from social situations and he grows progressively more reclusive. Eventually, Robbie's parents realize their son will never be able to function in the world beyond their front door. Furthermore, they worry because they know he will someday have to be institutionalized when they can no longer care for him.

All these cases are real, although the children's names have been changed to protect their identities. Some of them are students of Cheryl Rahaman, a special education teacher in New Paltz, New York.

In addition to devoting all her working hours to helping

children like Robbie and Frank and Rene, Rahaman is a wife and the mother of a twelve-year-old daughter. Together, the family breeds and shows Afghan Hounds, German Shepherd Dogs and Shi Tzus.

Therein lies the story of a lady who, with her dogs, is making small miracles that may someday become major contributions to society and the children she teaches. It is also the story of one particular dog, a big, heavy-coated German Shepherd Dog named Bay.

Rene Simpson was institutionalized after her mother's death. In the home, she was put into a class situation for the first time in her life. The description of her behavior reads like a nightmare. Testing and observations by the staff spelled it out in detail. She resisted attempts at communal activity, demonstrated severe anxiety and insecurity, spoke very little, could not convey original thoughts and totally rejected environmental stimuli. In addition, she exhibited auditory discrimination difficulty, was extremely distrustful of new situations and new people and refused to interact with her peers.

In short, Rene was locked within herself, unable to get out, to communicate with anyone, even to love or be loved. Her physical and environmental problems were so great that there appeared little hope she'd ever be much more than a senseless, mindless being, simply living out her days at the mercy of those around her.

Then Cheryl Rahaman entered her world. Rahaman came to Rene's classroom for ten days to observe her at her desk. During that period, Rene demonstrated great concern at the woman in the back of the room. She constantly needed reminders from her teacher to resume her work of adding and subtracting with paper cups or cutting out pictures or whatever simple tasks she was given. Rene frequently held her teacher's hand for reassurance that the passive observer was harmless.

Then one day, Rahaman brought with her the male German Shepherd Dog named Bay. The dog had been trained in advanced obedience and responded to voice and hand signals. Despite his size, he was gentle and quiet and accustomed to working with special children.

During Rene's classroom work, she had frequently

demonstrated an interest in pictures and stories of dogs. This particular affinity was the first clue that perhaps Rene could be stimulated and so Bay came to visit. As hoped, Rene immediately responded with a single-minded interest that none of her teachers had previously observed. Perhaps the dog could be used to unlock the windows of her mind and usher her into the world outside.

"Behavior modification," says Rahaman, "is essential for proper socialization of any living being incorporated into a society. Instinctive behavior is not always accepted behavior.

"Therefore, it becomes necessary to modify such behavior into a socially accepted form. Behavior modification is an integral part of the training of every social child regardless of his mental capabilities.

"Functionally retarded children of low socioeconomic backgrounds are usually the product of a poverty that yields a lonely insecurity and obscurity. In many cases the children of these homes begin their battle for recognition and stimulation from the moment they arrive home from the hospital. For most of their early development, these children grow up with their needs unattended."

On the second day with Bay, Rene stroked him continuously, running her fingers through his coat. Her teacher encouraged Rene to speak his name, but she refused. She declined to participate in any classroom project and remained locked in silence. She seemed content only to pet the big dog.

It wasn't until day three that the breakthrough occurred. And when it did, heaven opened up for the little girl who couldn't face the world in which she found herself.

It started out much like the previous days. Rene in her seat and Bay lying beside her as the child fondled him. "The teacher had arranged a series of flash cards with pictures of different breeds of dogs," recalls Rahaman. "Under each picture was the name of that breed. Rene was asked to repeat the names of the breeds aloud as her teacher flipped through the cards. However, Rene showed no reaction to the cards or the teacher throughout the activity."

Then, as the session came to an end, and with Rene still clinging to the dog, Rahaman called the dog to her saying, "Bay, come." The dog responded immediately.

As the dog went toward Rahaman, Rene realized she was about to be separated from her new friend. Suddenly, she blurted out, loud and clear, "Bay, come!" The dog whirled and raced back to the child. Rene threw her arms around the big dog's neck and buried her face in his fur.

For the first time in her life, Rene had called out to a living being other than her mother. And she was rewarded with love!

A subsequent typewritten study report of Rene and Bay states matter of factly: "The teacher and Rahaman developed a program using the dog as a prompt and reward to effectuate language in Rene."

Cold words, perhaps, to depict a moment of great triumph in the life of a human being. Rahaman explains it in more detail when she says, "The child who participates in his dog's socialization is attuned to the necessity of his own socialization. The program outlined for Rene was designed to reinforce the need for communication and social skills while providing her with the love and companionship of a dog."

Rene is not the only child Rahaman has reached through a dog. Take Jeffrey, for example. Rahaman tells about him with a special hint of extra-caring in her voice.

"Juvenile schizophrenia is another problem where dogs can be helpful. I have a documented case involving a neurologically impaired juvenile schizophrenic boy, named Jeffrey, who made significant strides with his Afghan Hound.

"As you know, juvenile schizophrenia is just that—juvenile. And as these children near adulthood, they usually enter a state of remission that, when handled properly, will carry them quite successfully through their adult years.

"In the case of this now young adult, he was able to substitute the emotional reenforcement he received from his puppy for the artificial mood elevators previously prescribed."

What Rahaman doesn't say is that Jeffrey lived in her home as a youngster. He is now a functioning, working member of society, living independently in his own apartment in a big city. He will forever be grateful to Rahaman and her Afghans for giving him the help he needed when he was a juvenile.

Speech impaired children are also candidates for canine therapy. "Because a dog responds to tone rather than actual words," expounds Rahaman, "a poor talker is quite apt to communicate well with a dog. The child can successfully convey his needs and emotions to a living, reciprocating being without the burden of frustration and censure attached to human conversation.

"In addition, clinics dealing in child psychology and the socialization of the mentally retarded have begun using dogs in their programs with many positive results."

Skeezer, for example, a mixed breed dog living in the Children's Psychiatric Hospital in Michigan, has been responsible for a number of breakthroughs. Most of the children there were reticent, reclusive and somewhat hostile. Skeezer fills a gap in the emotional security of these lonely, retarded children.

Many nights Skeezer can be found making the rounds at bedtime to say goodnight to the patients. Often, the dog provides a miraculous sedative to help a sad little child through the night.

Gar is another four-legged therapist at the hospital. A furry Norwegian Elkhound, the dog broke the barriers of communication and opened the door to learning for both the little six-year-old autistic girl and Frank, the psychotic, retarded boy. And there will be many more in the years ahead.

If educators and medical personnel are to help retarded and emotionally disturbed children learn to function in society, they, the people responsible for developing these children, must use every tool at their disposal to obtain positive results. It is becoming increasingly obvious that people like Cheryl Rahaman and her dog Bay are the ones who must lead these children out of the silence and the darkness of their minds.

Perhaps a line from "Children of the Silent Night," a documentary about handicapped children, says it most poignantly: "An ear finely tuned to nature, cannot help but hear the symphony of man."

The Invisible Handicap

Listen to the song of the white-throated sparrow. Hear the bacon crisping in the pan. Snuggle deep beneath the covers at the sound of rain on the roof. Sway to the rhythm of your favorite song. Alert to the staccato beat of a typewriter. Daydream to the lapping of waves upon the shore. Glow to the words of someone special saying, "I love you."

Now cover your ears and you lose them all. Not for just this moment. Forever. No more music. No more voices. No more sounds of nature. No more noise of life going on around you. Just silence. Eternal silence.

Now your other senses have to go into overdrive. You must be ever watchful lest you miss danger, life, busyness, learning, joy and—yes, even love. Be careful, pay attention or life will pass you by. For you are deaf, my friend, and most of those around you will never know it.

. . . .

That's just about how it is for the deaf. Young or old, deaf people are vulnerable, isolated, nervous. How can a person relax when he can't hear what's going on around him? It has been that way for them since the first deaf person walked the face of the earth.

But, now there is a way. The "way" is Hearing Ear dogs for the deaf. And Shorty is a perfect example of this unique group of canine companions.

The story of Shorty is also the story of Jenny Renaud, a tough, determined fighter who survived scarlet fever as a child—then, as an adult, deafness, epilepsy, alcoholism, chronic allergies and most recently pancreatitis and a six-week stay in Abington Memorial Hospital in Pennsylvania.

But it wasn't until April 1981 that her fight to survive all of these maladies and whatever else lies ahead in her future became bearable. For that's when Shorty joined her team and gave her not only the will to fight, but to win. Shorty is a Hearing Ear dog.

A three-year-old female dog of questionable heritage, Shorty looks more than a little like a combination of the collie, Lassie, and a canine Edward G. Robinson. In her role as Jenny Renaud's partner in life, Shorty can be as gentle and loving as Lassie or as tough and tenacious as the famed movie star.

Their union was no accident. Jenny has been struggling with her disabilities for most of her forty-five years. For the first thirty years, she underwent fifty-one ear operations in her fight against deafness.

Then, in 1968, a tragic automobile accident left her with epilepsy. Finally, in 1977, she was forced to accept the reality that the medical profession had exhausted every means to restore her hearing. She would be totally deaf in a matter of a few years and the deafness would be permanent.

The fear and frustrations of what the future held for her brought about the ultimate insult, alcoholism, to her already stressed body. She found herself in the Alcoholic Rehabilitation Center at Norristown, Pennsylvania, State Hospital. From there she was moved to Independence House, an alcoholic rehabilitation center, where she lived for another year.

Eventually, Jenny was ready once more to try life on her own. But, this time, she contacted International Hearing Dogs, Inc., in Henderson, Colorado. Yes, they did train dogs to assist the hearing impaired. Yes, she was eligible for a dog. And yes, they did have a dog for her.

It wasn't long before Jenny met Sandy Kilstrup, a trainer from International Hearing Dogs, Inc., and Shorty. Kilstrup and Shorty flew to Philadelphia where Jenny met them at the airport. For the next five days, Kilstrup trained Jenny to use all the behaviors that Shorty had been taught in her three months at the Colorado training center.

Jenny learned, for example, that Shorty would pester her every morning when the alarm clock rang. And she'd keep pestering until Jenny got up. No sleeping late when there's a Hearing Ear dog around.

Shorty, a Hearing Ear dog, checks the origin of the alarm clock's bell prior to waking up her mistress, Jenny Renaud. *Ken Parlini*

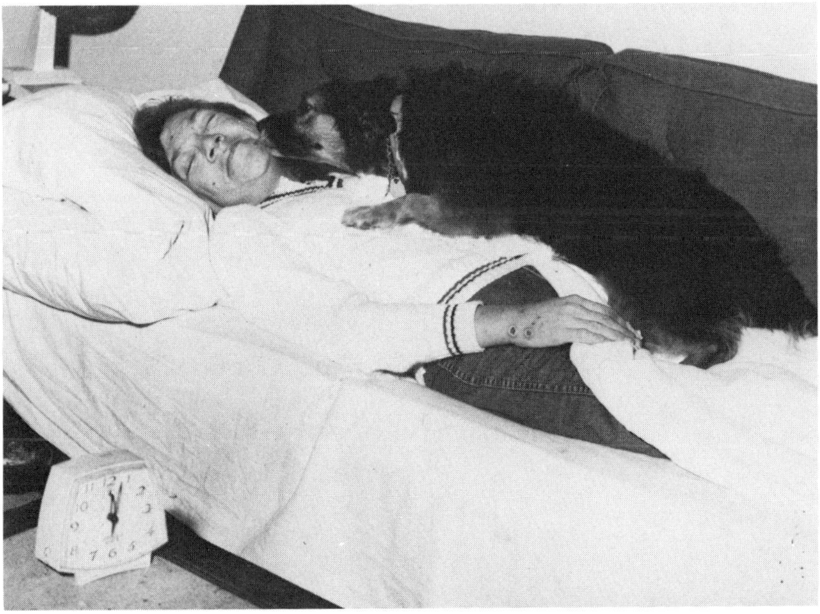

Hearing Ear dogs are trained to jump on their owners to wake them up at the sound of an alarm. *Ken Parlini*

When the doorbell rings, Shorty runs between Jenny and the door to indicate the presence of a visitor. *Ken Parlini*

Shorty had also been trained in a multitude of other behaviors as well. A knock on the door, for instance, finds Shorty racing back and forth between Jenny and the source of the knock. A smoke alarm elicits the same response. So do ringing telephones, babies crying, security buzzers buzzing, tea kettles whistling or a car pulling into the driveway. In short, a Hearing Ear dog becomes the ears of a deaf person.

As the ears of its master, the Hearing Ear dog goes wherever the master goes. To date, thirty-seven states have passed laws affording Hearing Ear dogs the same rights as Seeing Eye dogs. But until every state recognizes the value of Hearing Ear dogs, and the general public becomes accustomed to seeing these dogs as they assist their owners, life, at times, for the deaf masters will remain difficult.

One of the most difficult situations experienced by Jenny occurred in June 1982. Hospitalized with pancreatitis, Jenny had to send Shorty to her veterinarian to stay the duration. But, without her partner, Jenny's condition did not improve. Finally, her physician, Dr. Warren Mathew, got permission from the Abington Memorial Hospital officials to let Shorty stay with her owner in the hospital room.

That did the trick. Jenny's condition went from "status quo" to "improving rapidly" and six weeks later Jenny and Shorty went home to their apartment in Norristown.

Having to obtain special permission to stay together in the hospital, however, was not the only indignity suffered by Jenny and Shorty. They have been thrown off buses, out of supermarkets, asked to leave restaurants and even refused passage on the train between New York and Philadelphia. But, like we said, Jenny is a fighter.

With the help of her attorney, a bill was passed in the Pennsylvania Legislature that makes it illegal to refuse Hearing Ear dogs admittance to public places and sets a $200 fine for refusing that right. In addition, Hearing Ear dogs receive their annual licenses free of charge, wear bright orange collars and leads and their masters carry special cards with them saying that the dogs are certified Hearing Ear dogs.

Certification does not come with the dog. The owner and dog must earn the certified status by proving that they are, in fact, a working team. In the case of Shorty, a member of the

Board of Directors of International Hearing Dogs came to Jenny's home and observed the dog in action about six months after Shorty had taken up residence with her.

If the tester does not feel that the dog in question is truly replacing the auditory skills of its owner, it does not become certified. In that case, more work and training would have to be undertaken before certification would be granted.

Shorty had no difficulty being certified. She took her job seriously right from the start.

The dog not only compensates for Jenny's hearing impairment, she has assumed the role of protector as well. In traffic, Shorty pulls Jenny away from the sounds of moving vehicles and becomes very protective when her owner is approached by suspicious strangers either in public or at home.

But all this dedication and performance does not come without cost. First, International Hearing Dogs adopts specially qualified dogs from animal shelters. The candidates for hearing training must be healthy, happy, intelligent dogs and, most of all, anxious to please people. In this way, unwanted pets are saved from euthanasia and given second chances at living useful lives.

Next, the dog begins three months of training, which includes basic obedience and specialized behavior training. Once the potential new master is selected, the dog often receives additional training to meet the unique needs of the new owner.

Finally, a trainer flies the dog to the new home just as Sandy Kilstrup did with Shorty. Five days of intensive in-home training plus room and meals for the trainer add up to a final approximate cost from adoption to delivery of $2,800.

There is always a follow-up visit for certification and sometimes additional or review training is needed to keep the dog up to date on what is expected of him.

International Hearing Dogs places the dogs at no cost to the deaf. All funds for training and care come from private and group contributions.

Another organization that provides dogs trained in auditory awareness is The Hearing Dog Program. An offshoot of the American Humane Association, it also uses dogs acquired from animal shelters and gives them, free of charge, to hearing impaired and deaf people.

Although it began in Minnesota under sponsorship of the Society for Prevention of Cruelty, its official headquarters today is in California at the San Francisco Society for the Prevention of Cruelty to Animals. Because of the success of The Hearing Dog Program, the SPCA hopes to open training centers in other cities in the future.

Still another type of hearing assistance program comes from The Hearing Ear Dog Program at Bryant Hill Farm in Jefferson, Massachusetts. It is under the sponsorship of the New England Education Center.

There, amid the ninety acres and country atmosphere, new deaf owners spend two weeks with their dogs before they take the dogs home.

The dogs have been trained for three to five months in basic obedience and auditory awareness before they are matched to deaf people.

An organization official explains, "We feel very strongly that our two-week, facility-based schooling is the only way to go. It's the more expensive way, the more time-consuming way, but we have such a high success rate we can't imagine using any other method."

During the two-week stay the deaf person and dog learn to work as a team. They go on shopping trips together, eat together, live together. They practice all the things they will do when they return to their home. Perhaps the most important thing that the deaf person learns is that the dog is an extension of himself. And that extension translates to freedom.

It costs approximately $1,500 to develop a Hearing Ear dog. The deaf owner, however, pays only $150 as a token fee for the dog. The remainder of the cost is absorbed by private and group donations.

The United States is not the only country witnessing the development of assistance dogs for the deaf. In England, Peter Messent, an animal behaviorist with the Animal Studies Centre in Leicestershire, is currently planning a research program to study the effect of Hearing Ear dogs on recipients. The Royal National Institute for the Deaf is among those organizations managing the placement of Hearing Ear dogs.

Whether it be the United States, Europe, or anywhere else in the world, deaf people are indeed victims of an invisible handicap. And, as Jenny Renaud said in describing her feelings about Shorty, "She's given me all that medical science couldn't. There's a special bond between us that I can't explain. But most of all, she's given me freedom and love. What a wonderful gift!"

For Jenny Renaud, Shorty has become the "way." The way to live, love, laugh and have the freedom to enjoy life.

States with Hearing Ear Dog Laws*

1. Arkansas
2. Arizona
3. California
4. Colorado
5. Connecticut
6. Florida
7. Georgia
8. Illinois
9. Iowa
10. Kentucky
11. Maine
12. Maryland
13. Massachusetts
14. Michigan
15. Minnesota
16. Mississippi
17. Missouri
18. Montana
19. New Hampshire
20. New Jersey
21. New Mexico
22. New York
23. Nevada
24. North Carolina
25. Oklahoma
26. Ohio
27. Oregon
28. Rhode Island
29. South Dakota
30. Tennessee
31. Texas
32. Utah
33. Vermont
34. Virginia
35. Washington
36. West Virginia
37. Wisconsin

*Afford Hearing Ear dogs the same rights as Seeing Eye dogs.

Dogs and Autistic Children

The frail blond boy sat on the window seat rocking back and forth, a pillow clutched in his arms. Outside, the sun cast a chartreuse glow over the morning landscape, beckoning those inside to come out and celebrate the day.

The teacher approached the boy, placed a gentle hand on his shoulder and looked down, studying him. "If only I could help him," she prayed silently to an invisible diety. She felt the muscles tighten beneath her hand. Slowly, reluctantly, she withdrew her hand and turned away to go to another child.

The boy seemed not to notice the teacher or the scenery beyond the window pane. Instead, he stared into space as if there were nothing there. His ceaseless rocking never lost a beat.

Suddenly, a small tan dog, chasing a butterfly, ran across the lawn outside. The boy noticed. For a moment, the rocking stopped as he followed the dog's progress across the yard.

Shortly, the dog passed out of his view. Once more, the boy began rocking again. . . .

. . . .

Autism is a relatively new word that describes a very old disability. It was identified by a French physician as early as 1799. Today, the National Society for Autistic Children (NSAC) defines it on the cover of an informative booklet they use for distribution to the general public.

"Autism is a life-long brain disorder that prevents proper understanding of what a person sees, hears, or otherwise senses. It causes severe problems in learning, communication, and behavior."

Frank Warren, Executive Director of the NSAC, explained

in a recent letter, "Autism is a severe neurological disability which affects a person's ability to understand his surroundings—particularly the nuances of human interaction."

The word autism comes from the Greek word *autos,* meaning *self.* American child psychiatrist Leo Kanner first wrote about the syndrome in 1943 when he described these children as being withdrawn into themselves. The word autistic has remained ever since.

There is no accurate way to count the total number of autistic individuals in the world, but figures show there are about 340,000 autistic people in the United States today. Approximately 113,000 of these are children under the age of twenty-one. There are autistic people all over the world, of all races and all socioeconomic backgrounds.

At least three times as many boys are affected than girls and, almost without exception, autism begins at birth. Most autistic children suffer other abnormalities, such as severe central nervous system disorders, as well.

Although speech and language are absent or delayed in autistic children, their specific thinking capabilities may be present and functioning. Therein seems to lie the problem.

Take a child, for example, who can think and lock him up within his own body. His frustration at not being able to communicate, understand and learn must be terrifying. That's autism.

But there is a young woman in Newport Beach, California, who is finding a way to reach these children. Her name is Susan Myles and she's a pet-facilitated therapy consultant.

Myles began her therapy activities working with severely handicapped children at the Gill Education Center in Huntington Beach, California. Next, she took her now-famous Collies to nursing homes and homes for the aged where they brought happiness to the patients and opened up lines of communication between the staff and the patients.

In 1982 Myles—who is a member of the National Association of Dog Obedience Instructors, the Animal Behavior Society and has a degree in Wild Animal Training and Management—developed a program using dogs with autistic children in a public school in California that offers special education classes. The project began with seven children ranging in age from ten to thirteen years, a teacher, two aides and Myles.

"We used four pure-bred Collies," explains Myles. "The temperament traits that these particular Collies were bred for include an ability to generalize commands to anyone, a low activity level, gentleness with their bodies, low to medium vigor, low body sensitivity (maulability), indiscriminate friendliness, high resistance to stress introduced by changes and ability to tolerate many people handling them simultaneously."

The dogs had been introduced to children and various situations from age five weeks. They had all been trained to respond to voice and hand signals. In addition, they had grown up with crutches, canes, wheelchairs and walkers around their play yard, so they were prepared for any eventuality.

"The project was conducted over a ten-week period. Initially, we introduced one dog to the children. Most of the children had not been exposed to dogs, and I was worred about their reaction," recalls Myles.

"The dog was presented lying down and the children were encouraged to stroke its coat. A few of the children indicated immediate interest while others stood back and watched."

The attention span of autistic children is frequently short, making learning a problem. Within a few weeks, the four dogs were able to provide a focus for the children, thus giving them more concentration.

Eventually, the children began to relax and interact with the dogs. Four of them learned to mimic speech patterns, saying the dogs' names and pointing out various parts of the dogs' bodies.

"Walking the dogs around the room and signaling 'sit' was a real achievement for four of the children. They were able to focus on the dogs long enough to follow a simple sequence such as walking around the chair two times, walk past the table and signal 'sit.'

"As the weeks passed, the kids gave more definite signs of recognition each time the dogs came to class. Marie, one of the children, entered the project making unrecognizable sounds for words. By week five, she could sound out 'sit,' 'down,' and 'speak' well enough for the dogs to recognize and respond.

The child who is locked within himself can learn to express thoughts with the aid of a compassionate canine friend. *Ken Parlini*

A dog can help ease the autistic child's emotional difficulties.

"But the most memorable change came from Josh. He would engage in rocking back and forth whenever he was upset or startled and could not be stopped. This behavior is typical of autism. We noticed a gradual lessening of that behavior when the dogs were near him.

"By the fourth week, Josh ceased his rocking every time the Collies were near him. When the dogs were withdrawn, the behavior started again."

In addition to walking and talking with the dogs, the children learned how to roll the dogs from side to side and hold up hula hoops that the dogs would jump through. These behaviors helped to strengthen weak or spastic muscles and develop confidence in the children.

The results of the project were documented by Myles. In her conclusion she states, "We saw better attention spans, increased social contact with me (an unknown), better dexterity, increased mimicry and better speech in four of the children. Even the other three, who did not show dramatic accomplishments, exhibited a slight increase in attention span."

This pioneer project of using dogs to reach autistic children may be the forerunner of a movement to help the individual who is neurologically locked within himself break out of the prison of his own being. For, as Frank Warren said, autism affects the victim's ability to understand his surroundings, particularly the nuances of human interaction.

If that's the case, then perhaps man will realize that the successful interaction of autistic people with dogs may ultimately lead to successful interactions with their own species.

Dogs in Prisons

A hundred years ago, in the state of Washington, an Indian chief by the name of Seattle said, "What is a man without beasts? If all the beasts were gone, men would die from great loneliness of spirit, for whatever happens to the beast also happens to man. All things are connected. Whatever befalls the earth befalls the sons of the earth."

There is no greater loneliness of spirit than that suffered by those who have broken the rules of society and must pay for their deeds in prison. Even though for centuries our prisons have been generally overcrowded, they have always been lonely places.

They are ugly places, too. Ugly in the sense that the prison environment is filled with more crimes, such as intimidation, drugs, physical atrocities, emotional traumas, sexual perversion, and even murder.

Despite the general knowledge of these hideous conditions, society has been unsuccessful in its attempts to change things very much since medieval times. And the cost of this bad confinement of criminals is absolutely astounding.

Franklin Williams, a well-known radio commentator, recently presented an in-depth report on prisons in the United States. In his summary of prison conditions and the cost to the taxpayer, he made the statement that more money is spent on keeping a prisoner than sending a child to Yale or Harvard.

Today, however, society has begun to recognize the emotional, physical and spiritual debilitation of prison inmates and is acting, although haltingly at first, to remedy that problem. One of the most innovative programs in prison psychotherapy is taking place at Purdy Treatment Center for Women in Pierce County, Washington.

There, Dr. Leo K. Bustad, Dean of the College of Veterinary Medicine at Washington State University, and Kathy Quinn, a Tacoma photographer active in pet therapy, conceived the idea of having prisoners learn to train dogs to help the handicapped.

The pilot project began in the summer of 1982. There would be many benefits from the program. The prisoners would obtain on-the-job experience in dog training, learn about vocational opportunities in working with animals and, hopefully, learn how to alter their own behavior patterns as well.

As for the dogs, they would receive training in basic obedience that would make them more manageable and responsive to learning more sophisticated skills. They would also benefit from the socialization offered by a group of people other than those they already knew. Ultimately, their advanced lessons would make them ideal companions for wheelchair users, deaf people and elderly people who live alone.

Three days a week, for three and a half hours a day, instructors Kathy Quinn, Dawn Jecs and Marsha Henkel took six dogs to Purdy State Prison for Women. Henkel and Jecs did the instructing and Quinn recorded the progress of the dogs and inmates.

At first twelve volunteer inmates were chosen. Three of the inmates were serving long-term sentences, one a life term. Most of the volunteers were young women with children. One inmate, at nineteen, was barely past childhood herself.

The group worked in a large gymnasium with an adjoining fenced baseball field. Handlers and dogs worked outdoors when the weather was nice and indoors when it wasn't. During each session there was time for each handler to become acquainted with the dog she was training. They could walk around together, play fetch with the dog, or just lie in the grass and make friends with each other.

Quinn recalls the prisoners' first reactions to the new experience. "Some of the inmates broke down and cried at having physical contact with a warm, living creature again."

As for prison officials, they were skeptical at first. They were concerned about the safety of the inmates, the dogs and the instructors. They were reluctant to support the program, but when they saw the prisoners' response to the dogs and the training, they reversed their attitude.

The dogs used were Doberman Pinschers, Shetland Sheepdogs, Corgis, English Cocker Spaniels, Irish Setters, an Australian Cattle Dog, a Schipperke and a mixed breed. In the pilot program, all dogs had been previously trained. Some had earned obedience titles and were owned by the instructors. All were eager to please.

One of the most poignant moments in the program came on the first day of training. When the inmates saw the Doberman Pinschers, they expressed fear of the dogs. "Doberman Pinchers are mean and will turn on you," they said. "Never turn your back on them."

When Quinn heard that remark, she responded with, "It's funny you would say that for that's exactly what people in the community said to us about *you* when they found out we were going to take the dogs to prison." With that remark, the prisoners forever loved the Dobermans.

As the training program developed and the inmates became more comfortable with their charges, they began to experience more confidence in themselves. They spent time each day talking with the instructors about jobs in the field of animals and their own futures. Some expressed interest in animal-related jobs; others said they would like to become professional dog trainers. One woman, scheduled for release in the near future, is considering becoming an animal technician for a veterinarian. The life-term prisoner is anxious to begin a full-time career in prison of training dogs to help the handicapped.

The pilot program was an overwhelming success. Plans for a full-time program have already begun. Kennels must be built at the prison to house dogs in training. A staff of long-term prisoners will be assigned to feed and care for the dogs. Another six will become full-time trainers. Classes will be offered to teach animal-related jobs to other inmates.

"Funding for the program," says Dr. Bustad, "could come from the public and the community. And we hope the program will become a regular part of Washington State University's nonprofit People-Pet-Partnership Program."

As for the inmates, one life-term woman said it best. "We look forward to the chance of helping disabled people. And there's another reason: The animals love us no matter what we've done."

Prisoners training dogs to serve the handicapped is not the only activity using dogs in prisons. Dogs are helping the criminally insane, too. At the Lima, Ohio, State Hospital, David Lee has been using pets as part of the patients' rehabilitation program for some time now. Lee reports results have been amazing.

Psychotherapists Samuel and Elizabeth Corson, from Ohio, have discovered the value of pet-facilitated therapy in working with emotionally disturbed patients. Some of them, with intractable mental illnesses, have made remarkable improvement.

In an institution for the criminally insane, pets have reversed the trend of some of the patients to become reclusive. The men responded to the pets, assumed full care of the animals and regained awareness of their own environment.

Best of all, the pets served to establish a feeling of trust for the hospital staff. Once trust for the staff developed, a line of communication emerged whereby the inmates could benefit from treatment.

Dr. Bustad examined prison psychotherapy programs in Melbourne, Australia. "Prisoners there," he reports, "train guide dogs for the blind."

One of the most important needs for the elderly and the disabled in the United States could be met by prisoners, Bustad suggests. "Trained dogs can act as retrievers for people in wheelchairs, as 'ears' for the deaf. They also can provide security and companionship for the elderly and lonely."

Whatever the final outcome of prisoners training dogs to serve mankind, whatever behaviors they teach the dogs, whatever vocations they learn as a result of their new-found interests in animals and dogs in particular, one thing is sure. The prisoners will build confidence in their own abilities. And when one realizes one's own capabilities, one can experience self-esteem. This, in turn, diminishes a loneliness of spirit and develops appreciation for Chief Seattle's idea that "whatever happens to the beast also happens to man."

Snow is carefully removed from the body of a young hunter who became lost during a sudden winter storm. *unknown*

Gentle Giants of the Lost

His jaws can bite at seven hundred pounds per square inch. His powerful paws can rip open in seconds a package labeled "securely wrapped" by United Parcel. His radar-equipped ears can identify the slightest rustle of leaves or the step of a slippered foot a half-mile away. His brown eyes can pierce the thick bush to see the faintest movement overlooked by his master. His firm back and short, heavy-boned legs can carry him for miles without so much as a pant at his destination point.

He can be a loving friend, a guide to the blind, a keeper of flocks, a lethal guardian of men and equipment. To members of a rescue dog team, he is worth a hundred human searchers and twice as fast. He is a German Shepherd Rescue Dog. He is the gentle giant of the lost.

. . . .

The story of Search and Rescue Dogs is a little known story simply because there are very few of them and the handlers of those dogs don't talk about their work very much. They're a self-contained, quiet group. They practice their skills, work hard and find reward for their efforts in the end result of their searches.

Rescue Dogs can be found in many countries of the world. In Europe, Austria for example, they are known as Avalanche Dogs and are used to find people buried under tons of snow following natural disasters such as avalanches. In the rugged mountains of the western United States, some of the Rescue Dogs are trained to work avalanches also.

The majority of Rescue Dogs in the United States are trained to find lost people: children who wander away from campsites, old people who become disoriented and wander away from their homes, hunters who collapse from hypothermia in the woods, murder victims whose bodies are dismembered and buried in shallow graves in farm fields and wooded areas.

Whatever the reason for a person becoming lost, the same principle for locating that person is used. A person's body, dead or alive, emits certain scents that rise into the air in the form of gases. The gases become part of the air flow around the source and thereby form a cone-shaped indicator to the dog.

Imagine a cone turned upside down. Close to the source the cone is narrow and the scent is strong. As the scent rises from the source, the scent cone becomes wider and weaker. As the scent joints the air flow above it, it travels at the same rate of speed as the breeze.

The longer the source, or in this case the lost person, remains in one place the more heavily scented the air around him becomes. Because Rescue Dogs are trained to locate people by air-scenting, they have little difficulty detecting specific airborne scents of human beings. They are not affected by the scent of searchers who, more often than not, have combed an area prior to the dogs' arrival. Even the scents of sun-dried ground, rain, snow or other variables in weather-related conditions or terrain do not deter the dogs from their work. What's more, they don't even rely on smelling an article previously handled by the lost person. They search only for the scent of the victim.

In the United States, the American Rescue Dog Association (ARDA) is a national organization consisting of six rescue units throughout the country. Their members use large, gentle German Shepherd Dogs who have passed rigid tests of temperament and physical ability. Once accepted, the dogs undergo approximately two thousand hours of field training.

The handlers are highly trained in wilderness navigation, hazardous climate survival, first aid and evacuation skills. In addition, they receive formal and field training in search methods. Together, dogs and handlers participate in actual searches with other teams within their unit. Finally, each handler must purchase his own specialized equipment, which can cost up to $2,000.

When a handler and dog become certified to participate in legitimate searches, they are prepared not only to search for lost people, but to survive life in the wilderness themselves.

Marilyn Greene, Field Operations Director and past president of the Adirondack Unit of ARDA, comments on the extensive training given to all dogs and handlers.

"How do you train a dog to work twelve hours a day for three days and be just as effective in the last hour as the first? Proper positive motivation is the only way to gain the keen working capabilities of the search and rescue dog. Air-scent training is a complex process of motivation, manipulation and handler skill. It is the most difficult form of dog training attempted.

"ARDA dogs and handlers have an eighty-six percent success record on extended searches where all previous methods have failed."

Sadly, about ninety percent of the lost people found by ARDA teams are dead. They die of exposure to the elements and their environment, natural causes, accidents and sometimes suicide. ARDA members, however, never give up. They always hope the next search will result in a happy ending.

One search undertaken by the Adirondack Unit resulted in just such a happy ending and is recalled by Greene.

"The unit received a call one snowy December afternoon from an agency housing and caring for retarded adults. A middle-aged resident, clad only in pajamas and bedroom slippers, had wandered away from the facility, which bordered several extensive wooded areas. With much snow on the ground and darkness near, the team of three dogs and their handlers responded within the hour of the call for help.

"The facility was a circus of cars, trucks, firemen, foot searchers and snow mobiles. They had been combing the buildings, the grounds and the surrounding woods for hours. But as darkness approached, they realized they were not going to be successful before nightfall.

"When our unit arrived, we interviewed employees of the home and plotted areas to be searched on topographical maps. One dog and handler were sent into each area.

"Richard Dennis and his dog Dagmar, from Shirley, Massachusetts, were sent into the wooded area directly at the rear of the residential building. Snow was falling heavily and Dick reported the area filled with the footprints of previous

Marilyn Green evaluates a search area by helicopter. *Steve Youngentob*

Search and Rescue dogs pose for a group photo during an obedience exercise. *unknown*

searchers, but Dagmar worked enthusiastically, ignoring the footprints.

"They were approaching a stream when Dagmar alerted, jumped the stream, and proceeded over a small hill. Reaching the top of the hill, Dennis saw Dagmar on the slope pawing at a mound of snow. As the handler neared the mound, he saw two slippered feet.

"At first, Dennis thought the man was dead because of the way in which the snow had just piled up on top of him. But when Dennis brushed the snow from the victim's face, the man opened his eyes and spoke in a feeble voice, 'Is it time to go back now?'

"The man surely wouldn't have survived the night. His socks were frozen to his feet and he was rapidly moving into a serious state of hypothermia. Dennis assured the victim it was, indeed, time to go, and shortly the evacuation team carried him out of the woods to a waiting ambulance."

One of the main reasons why so little is known about Search and Rescue Dog teams is the fact that the members prefer to work without publicity, particularly in regard to individual dogs and handlers. They feel locating a lost person is a team effort and, without the backup support of the entire unit, success would be unattainable.

In short, it is not just a matter of a person and a dog wandering around field and forests hoping to stumble upon the victim. There's a highly trained, extremely sophisticated operation that goes into action once a call is received.

Upon arrival at a site, a base camp is immediately set up. The base camp is the heart of the search operation and from it the Operational Leader together with other unit members interview individuals involved, decide on a course of action, divide the site into search grids, and assign individual dog/handler teams to each grid.

While these vital steps are being taken, the Base Camp Operator is setting up a network of communications between handlers, base camp and local fire and police officials. In other words, preparation is immediately begun to send support groups out for evacuation once the victim is located. Taking time to prepare in advance can mean the difference between saving a victim once he's been found and losing him to

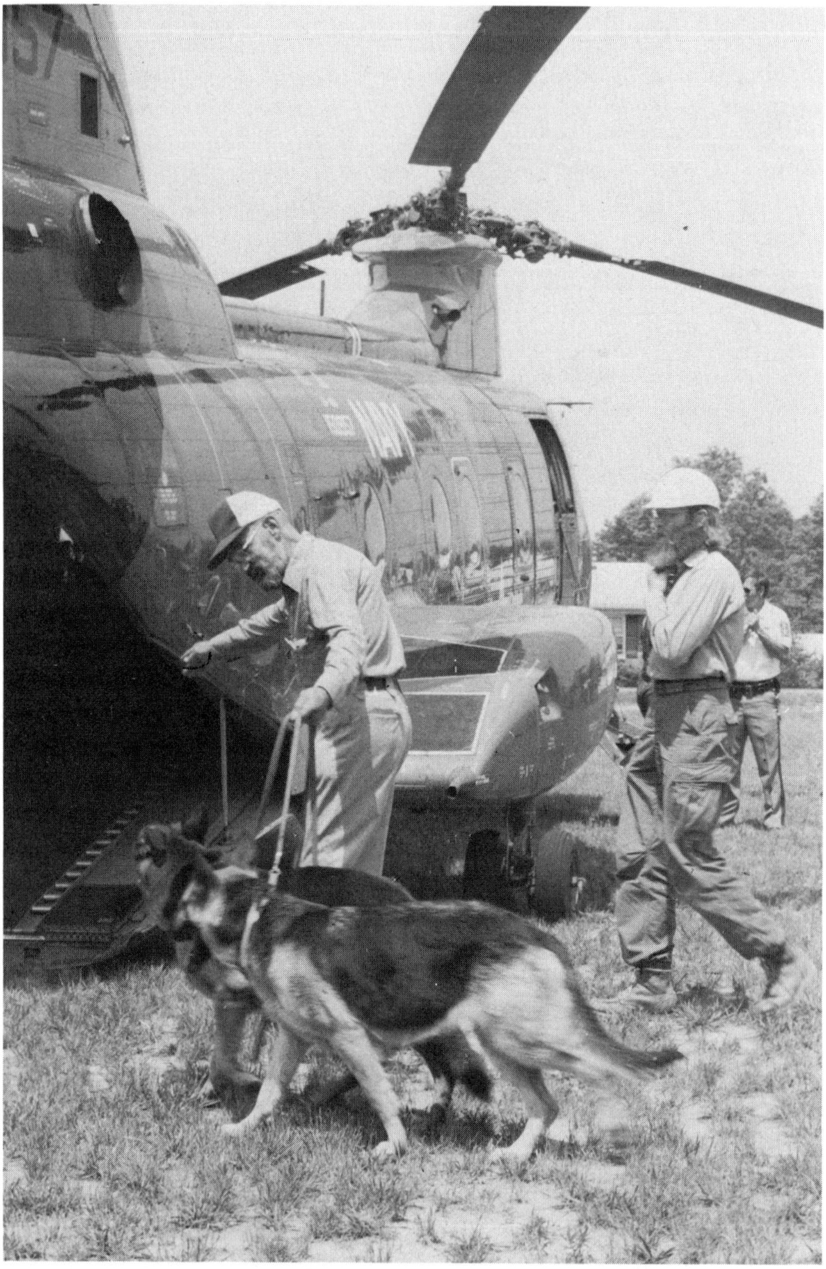

Robert Mackenzie and William Vought directing two Search and Rescue dogs into a helicopter in Westmoreland, Virginia, after a successful search mission.
Marilyn Greene

hypothermia and other natural causes because rescue facilities were not ready when needed.

Once the rescue operation is ready, dogs and handlers are sent into the field. Even then they are not alone, for they keep in constant touch with the base camp by radio. Yet with all the men and equipment, it is the dogs who must use their olfactory abilities to lead their masters to the victim. No wonder the men and women of Search and Rescue Dog teams are reluctant to point the finger of achievement toward an individual team. Without each member doing his own job to the best of his ability, there would be no story to tell.

The work performed by ARDA is so valuable and the number of qualified dog/handler teams so small, the United States Air Force Rescue Service regularly flies them beyond their home states to assist in major searches. They respond to any requesting agency anywhere in the United States and Alaska. Their National Alerting Phone is based in Seattle, Washington, and is 206-282-1177. Search alert phone numbers for the individual ARDA units can be found in the Directory at the back of this book. In addition, the Directory lists phone numbers for other independent individuals and organizations specializing in search and rescue work.

ARDA units participate in anywhere from ten to forty major searches per year. Although there are only about twenty qualified Search and Rescue Dog teams in the United States today, every one of them is dedicated to using their skills to save lives and recover lost people regardless of the circumstances under which they become lost. The gentle four-legged giants will remain the backbone of this operation and the hope of those who, for whatever reason, have lost their way.

PART III

Service Dogs

The Komondor, which originated in Hungary, was bred to guard flocks of sheep and is used today in the United States for the same purpose. Notice the similarity between the dog and the sheep. *Ken Parlini*

Herding and Guarding Dogs

The story of herding and guarding dogs in America is an Old World story with a New World twist that's a book in itself. Filled with good guys and bad guys, it's as rugged a tale as the geographical region from which it comes. And, like most stories of man and nature, it claims its share of heroes.

Livestock herding and guarding dogs have been used for thousands of years in countries the world over. Most of Europe, the British Isles, Russia, as well as Australia and Asia have produced and used these dogs since man began keeping flocks of sheep and herds of cattle.

Regardless of country of origin, the dogs seem to share certain similarities. First, they are "naturals." They come from long lines of working ancestors that have willed them their business-like natures. They are confident, independent, aloof to strangers. The herders can move hundreds of head of livestock from one range to another across rough terrain, through rushing waters, over rocky foot hills without losing an animal. The guarders can protect a whole flock of sheep overnight without losing one lamb to a predator.

Second, many of these dogs look like the animals they live with. Take, for example, the Komondor from Hungary. He's a dog of 75 to 125 pounds, has long shaggy cords of hair that hang to the ground and in color is very like the off-white of the sheep he guards. His dense coat provides him with an armor that is almost impenetrable to the teeth of predators.

Third, dogs of the working stock breeds seem able to cope with the extremes of weather. They can run the cattle through winter's worst blizzard, keep the sheep together in the hottest noon of August and work the stock with single-minded determination in torrential rains.

Perhaps the most amazing aspect of these dogs is that the casual observer must look very carefully before he even sees a dog among the herd. In short, they are not noticeably obvious, yet every animal knows they're there.

The training of both herding and guarding dogs starts when they are very young. As puppies they mingle with the animals they will be living with. Some even suckle the dams of the flock.

They learn to respond to the herdsman. They learn to circle the animals and yet keep an eye on their master. They learn the ways of the sheep and cattle. They learn to recognize the scent and sight of predators, both human and animal.

Ed Emmanuel, a stockman from Butler, Indiana, said it best when he commented, "There are only a few things that stock dogs need to know, but they need to know them WELL."

Herders learn to move large groups of animals from one place to another without letting individuals wander away or get lost. Guarders learn to lie quietly while the animals graze, yet be ever alert to the threat of predators whether they be a pack of wild dogs, coyotes, wolves or rustlers.

Since sheep and cattle represent millions of dollars worth of food, shelter, clothing and cash to Americans, the dogs that herd and guard these animals are valuable assets to all stockmen. Whether they are ranchers, shepherds, farmers or breeders, they have always appreciated the natural abilities of their canine assistants.

Some of the most popular breeds of herding and guarding dogs are listed here for those who might wish to do more research on the dogs that work with stockmen.

Herding Dogs

Australian Cattledogs – Queensland Blue Heelers
Australian Kelpies
Australian Shepherds
Belgian Sheepdogs
Border Collies
Catahoula Leopard Cowdogs (Hogdogs)
English Shepherds
Tervurens
Texas Blue Heelers

Guarding Dogs

Anatolian Shepherd dogs
Great Pyrenees
Karabash
Komondor
Kuvasz
Maremma
Shar Planinetz

The Old World story of dogs working with stockmen is a tradition of young dogs learning from older ones. They were bred and born on the range where their ancestors lived and worked. The men they worked with and the animals they herded and guarded were a way of life for them. And they were good at what they did.

In the New World, herding and guarding dogs have been welcomed by conservationists and stockmen alike. By stockmen because one or two dogs can do what it would take a dozen men to do, and by conservationists because the dogs obviate the use of poisons and other environmentally hazardous materials.

Lorna and Raymond Coppinger, from Montague, Massachusetts, have established a Livestock Dog Project to study the effectiveness of certain breeds of guarding dogs on ranches in the United States. Another study has been undertaken at the Wildlife Research Center in Denver, Colorado, to observe the effectiveness of Komondorok on predators in this country. Both studies are aimed at a better understanding of how to keep predators away from livestock by the use of dogs.

Earthquake Dogs

Nowhere is the renaissance of the man-dog phenomenon more exciting than the possibilities that exist in earthquake prediction by animals including dogs. Yet the signs of it go back as far as the fourth century B.C. For the twenty-four centuries between then and now, man had chosen to either ridicule or ignore it.

Precognitive behavior is simply the way in which animals respond to the release of ions, or charged particles from the ground, which occurs hours or even days before an earthquake. Since animals are more sensitive to their environment than man, they can and do react abnormally prior to earthquakes. Now, it seems, man has finally realized he can learn from the animals.

European archives document the fact that, in the fourth century B.C., snakes, rodents and small animals fled from the city of Helice in Greece before it was demolished. In 1755, birds and animals in Lisbon, Portugal, fled just prior to the earthquake that claimed so many lives there.

In the mid-1960s China organized the National Earthquake Prediction Bureau. Headed by a team of noted scientists using seismic recorders, the group is made up of over 100,000 citizens who have volunteered to report animal precognitive behavior. When the animal signs and the seismic readings increase in a given area, the bureau releases an earthquake alert and evacuates the area in question.

Although there have been many false alarms, the program has saved at least 100,000 lives. Most notable among the successful predictions was the evacuation of thousands of people from Haicheng, China, before a major earthquake leveled the city.

In the United States, SRI International, an independent organization that does contract research for the government and private business, has organized "Project Earthquake Watch." The project consists of over 1,500 volunteer observers of animal behavior in California. Over 250 species are observed regularly and reported on weekly.

Dr. Leon Otis, Director of the Psychobiology and Physiology Department at SRI, and his co-investigator, Dr. William Kautz, are trying to prove, once and for all, whether or not unusual animal behavior is a predictor of major earthquakes.

Dr. Kautz explained in the Winter 1982 edition of *The Latham Letter* that many changes occur in the environment just prior to most earthquakes. Since animals are thousands of times more sensitive than man or machines to certain physical stimuli, perhaps they are the best indicators of imminent earthquakes.

House pets, farm animals and even wild animals are being observed for strange behavior, such as rats fleeing their burrows, reptiles coming out of hibernation, dogs howling and becoming jumpy, horses and cows straining at their tethers. Even fish become frenzied and birds fly erratically.

Professor Helmut Tributsch, from Berlin's Free University, began studying this phenomenon in 1976 when he observed the devastation to a small village in the Italian Alps following an earthquake. Townspeople there reported to him the strange and unexplained behavior of their animals prior to the earthquake. It was then the professor began his own research.

Tributsch believed that positive ions are produced by rocks when they are placed under great pressure, and positive ions are what create the feelings of suspended animation and irritability in animals. This in turn causes animals, which are more sensitive than man to their environment, to act in a disturbed manner.

Eventually Tributsch announced his theory of positive ions. He also suggested a procedure of observation and evacuation similar to the one employed in China. Tributsch's book, *When the Snakes Awake* (MIT Outing Club Press), documents his case for animal prediction of earthquakes. And recently laboratory geologists at the University of Arizona proved his theory correct.

The United States Geological Survey, which is funding Project Earthquake Watch, is still in need of volunteer Californians who live in seismically active areas. Anyone wishing to participate in the project may do so by contacting project personnel. Their address is listed in the Directory at the back of this book.

Dr. Tributsch feels that man, unlike other animals, has lost a certain capacity to experience physiochemical signals in the world around us. But perhaps, if we are as wise as we seem to think we are, we can regain some of that cognition if we will only become more aware of the animals with whom we share this universe. At least, this renaissance appears to be giving us a second chance.

Police K-9 Dogs

The night came on like gangbusters, turning the warm October day into a chilly fall evening. And with it, the fog rolled in. Fog that crept into alleys and swirled under street lights and bounced auto headlights around like so many ping pong balls in a lottery machine.

But the city hardly noticed. It continued its usual activities of workers going home, buses heading for the barn and children leaving the streets and playgrounds to the creatures of the night.

One of the creatures was a man, twenty perhaps, dressed in an old Army jacket and blue jeans, who slinked along the rough brick wall of a building until he reached an alley. Hesitating to look down the narrow access lane, he pulled a ski cap further down on his head and put a hand to his pocket, checking.

The shoe store would be closing now and the owner would be counting his day's receipts. A quick hit and he'd have enough money to insure his "angel dust" habit for several days.

But fate had other plans this night. Out of the fog a patrol car pulled up alongside the man. Instinctively the police officer inside recognized trouble when he saw it. He stepped out of the car leaving the window open, the motor running and the dog inside alerted.

The young man turned and, almost as if he were part of a slow-motion movie, stepped toward the lawman. As he did, his hand reached up to his pocket, his face turned grim.

The dog saw the hand too, and responded. He leaped through the car window toward the suspect.

While the big German Shepherd Dog vaulted in mid-air, the black night turned red, then white-hot as the suspect's revolver exploded. The initial burst was answered within a

A police K-9 dog being trained to respond to hand signals by his officer/handler.
Captain Haggerty's School for Dogs

Disaster Dog locating people buried under debris following an explosion.
Captain Haggerty's School for Dogs

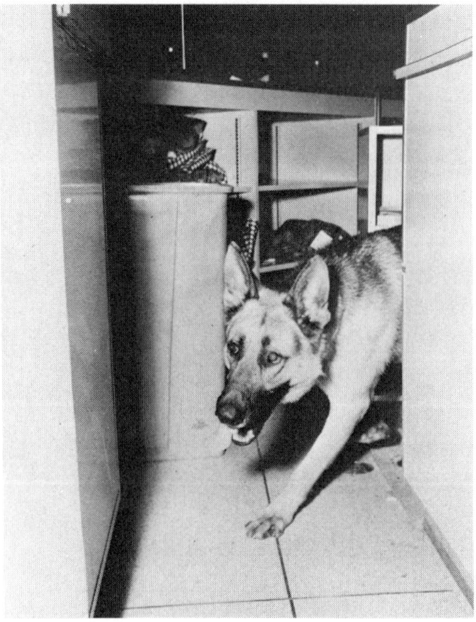

A Building Search Dog at Work.
Captain Haggerty's School for Dogs

millisecond by another explosion. The city street became Vietnam with the sounds of gunfire, screams, bodies falling and then, as quickly as it had begun, it was over.

The suspect lay like some discarded rag doll on the sidewalk, his life and his craving for drugs gone forever. Nearby lay the still body of the city's newest hero, a police K-9 dog named Fritz.

As the officer stood over the two bodies, the fog rolled in around them, shrouding the ugliness of the moment from the eyes peering out of the window across the street. In the distance police sirens screamed closer and closer as if echoing the final wail of the officer's fallen partner.

. . . .

Law enforcement agencies in states, counties, cities and towns from the Atlantic to the Pacific use K-9 dogs to augment their forces. The dogs are often donated by members of the community. Some are acquired from shelters. Most are German Shepherd Dogs.

All are highly trained professionals, each claiming a badge number just like their human partners. By the time police K-9 dogs complete three or four months of intensive training and hit the streets for patrol duty, they are so dedicated to their masters they will give up their lives to protect the officers.

Being dedicated to its master, however, isn't enough to qualify a dog to become a member of a police K-9 corps. He must be good at what he does and do it one hundred percent of the time. For if a dog is trained to do a specific job and he's not reliable, he can cause more problems than he can prevent. For example, if a dog is trained to perform building searches, he could overlook a hidden bomb that might explode. A prisoner escort dog, not paying attention to his charge, could allow a felon to escape and jeopardize a whole community.

The value of these dogs is not something one can estimate. A long-time police sergeant recently said that one good dog is worth ten men. Another sergeant on the New York State Police Force recently stated that it took four men five hours to search a building where a visiting dignitary was expected, while one dog can do it in a matter of minutes.

Although each K-9 school has designed its own training

program to meet the needs of the communities it serves, most have approximately the same basic curriculum and methods. The average course is about four months in duration.

The dogs begin training in basic obedience including response to both voice commands and hand signals. During this period they begin to build the bond with their handlers that will carry them through many rough situations in the months and years ahead.

Agility is another major subject. Building the body as well as the mind, agility work teaches the dog to get in and out of places and situations that he will face once he hits the street. The dog learns to jump through windows, climb ladders, negotiate cat walks, scale walls and crawl through narrow tunnels such as sewer pipes. In short, he becomes a highly skilled athlete.

Guard and attack work are next. He learns to bite and hold his victim. He learns to "out," or let go when told by his handler.

He learns to protect his officer/handler at the cost of his own life. He also learns to act on his own when his handler is unaware of impending danger. He learns to guard a suspect once the officer has placed that person under arrest.

Searching for hidden weapons, narcotics and lost or escaped persons is another job the K-9 dog must master. At first he learns to use his nose to find something he wants, such as a stick or old rag. The transfer to more serious tracking and scent work comes slowly and without force. Each time the dog is introduced to a new phase of scent training, he is encouraged to enjoy the exercise and succeed at it before moving on to the next more difficult step. Eventually, he learns how to indicate to his handler what and where he smells.

Throughout the training, the bond between dog and handler grows until they become a team. The dog learns when he's working and when he's not. In many cases, the dog lives at home with the officer and gets exposure to normal domestic situations as well as law enforcement work. He learns how to handle himself in both environments.

The versatility of K-9 dogs is perhaps the most interesting thing about them. They are the canine world's jacks-of-all-trades, and each dog, in his own specialty, is a master at what he does best. Listed below are some of the jobs performed by police K-9 dogs.

Sgt. Gerald Frye of the Arkansas City (Kansas) Police Department looks on encouragingly as Tami pulls herself up the twelve foot scaling wall during training. *Captain Haggerty's School for Dogs*

Crowd Control. These dogs walk calmly beside their masters amid large gatherings to assure the peaceful conduct of the crowd. You see them at rallies, football and baseball games, wherever people gather for rock concerts. They are trained to break up fights and subdue rowdy demonstrators. They never act without command unless their masters are threatened.

Patrol/Attack/Apprehension. They ride patrol cars and act as back-ups for officers who need help. They assist in the apprehension of felons and guard the suspects until the officer can obtain additional assistance.

Disaster Search. In the event of disaster, such as the collapse of a building or a major fire, these dogs move among the wreckage in search of victims. They don't touch the victims, but simply lead officers to the location of victims.

Lost Persons and Dead Bodies. These dogs are used in murder cases where a body has not been found. They are also used in locating lost persons, dead or alive.

Tracking and Trailing. Escaped felons and prisoners have slim chances of avoiding capture when a good tracking and/or trailing dog is put on their trail. A tracking dog follows, with or without prior scent, a precise path of the person he's tracking. A trailing dog takes the scent of the person and leads his handler over the most direct route to the person. The trailing dog uses air flow to determine the location of the person being sought.

Narcotics/Weapons/Evidence/Explosives. Dogs trained in these behaviors have highly developed olfactory systems that can tell them precisely where the object in question is located. Furthermore, they are trained to indicate to their handlers where these items are so the handlers can retrieve them. To prevent accidents to the dogs, most are not permitted to retrieve the articles themselves. Many times weapons searches are conducted to obtain evidence in criminal cases.

Protection. All police K-9 dogs are trained in the personal protection of their handlers. Without that dedication to their officer-handlers, they would not have the single-minded determination to perform their regular tasks.

Building Search. There are several reasons for building searches by dogs. First, drugs and various explosives and weapons are often hidden in buildings. The dogs are trained to go from room to room in search of unwanted articles. Building

A Doberman Pinscher being trained with a mannequin. The dog will be on guard duty in a New York department store.

Captain Haggerty's School for Dogs

searches are also conducted by police looking for escaped prisoners and felons. In addition, many buildings are searched routinely before the police will allow visiting dignitaries to enter them.

Smoke Detectors. Some K-9 dogs are trained to locate the source of smoke and alarm their handlers. This behavior is particularly helpful in the early identification of fires in particularly hazardous areas, such as industrial sites.

Prison Guard Dogs. These dogs are usually the bite-now-and-ask-questions-later type. When a prisoner scales a wall or climbs a fence there is usually no objective other than escape at the root of his action. And he must face a biting dog before he can reach freedom.

Demonstrations. There is no better way to show adults and children how gentle and trustworthy K-9 dogs can be than to use them in public demonstrations. Taking K-9 dogs into schools helps to demonstrate to children how their police department is prepared to protect them regardless of the threat to their own safety and well-being.

The cost of training and maintaining police K-9 dogs is miniscule compared to the job these dogs do for their communities. The feeling of security they evoke in the citizens is priceless. Yet the strongest image they create is the one perceived by the criminal element, that they are a stalwart backup to our men in blue.

Bovine Estrus Detection Dogs

A Miniature Schnauzer in New Jersey and a German Shepherd Dog in Texas are among a small, select group of dogs pioneering a project designed to save dairy farmers millions of dollars each year. The Miniature Schnauzer sits on a platform attached to the top of a three-foot stepladder as cows pass her on their way to the milking machines. The German Shepherd Dog moves down a three-and-a-half-foot platform situated directly behind three stalls, each containing a cow. One of the cows is in estrus, the other two are in diestrus.

Both dogs are searching for cows in season. When the Miniature Schnauzer detects a cow in estrus, she lies down. When the German Shepherd Dog identifies the estrus cow among the three, he sits behind the cow.

Detecting the peak copulation period in cows is one of the most difficult tasks a dairyman has to perform because there are no outward signs of estrus. Without breeding the cows when they come into estrus, they go dry and stop producing milk

A cow comes into season every twenty-one days and is only in season and breedable for somewhere between eight to twenty-four hours. Given such a short breeding period, there is no room for guesswork in the bovine breeding program.

When one considers that, in today's economic state, it costs two dollars per day per cow for maintenance, if a farmer misses a breeding opportunity on just a few cows and must wait another three weeks before the opportunity presents itself again, this becomes a costly problem and one which cries out to be solved.

In the late 1970s people, individually and in groups, began to realize that dogs could possibly be the answer to the problem. Since there are no visible signs of bovine estrus, they reasoned that dogs could be taught to recognize the physiological change that occurs in cows in estrus. They came to this conclusion because observers of sexual behavior in cattle felt that bulls use olfactory cues to determine when a cow is in estrus.

The United States Department of Agriculture at Beltsville, Maryland, did some research to determine if there was, in fact, a specific odor peculiar to cows during estrus. In 1978, the Reproduction Laboratory there published a paper by researchers C. A. Kiddy, D. S. Mitchell, D. J. Bolt and H. W. Hawk. Entitled "Detection of Estrus-Related Odors in Cows by Trained Dogs," the paper presented descriptions of a series of seven experiments using bovine vaginal fluid, urine and live cows. Some of the experiments were conducted in a laboratory, others on actual farms.

Four German Shepherd Dogs and two Labrador Retrievers were used. All the dogs came from the U.S. Department of Defense Dog Center at Lackland Air Force Base, Texas.

Each experiment contained multiple sessions and hundreds of trials within each session. The conclusion proved there is a definite odor in estrus cows that is absent in proestrus and diestrus bovines.

Armed with the knowledge that cows in season do emit a specific odor during periods of estrus, Drs. Kiddy and Mitchell began a second study to determine precisely when the odor first appears and how long it lasts.

For this project, they used three German Shepherd Dogs that had previously participated in the 1977 project and one Catahoula Leopard Cowdog. "All of the estrus odor detection dogs were trained at Southwest Research Institute and then sent to the United States Department of Agriculture's Agricultural Research Center at Beltsville, Maryland," explains Mitchell.

As before, some of the experiments were conducted in the laboratory and some outdoors. The dogs proved, once again, the value of their olfactory abilities. Their responses to the odor on the day of estrus were a surprising 94 percent correct.

In 1981 the researchers published a paper in the *Journal of Dairy Science* titled, "Estrus-Related Odors in Cows: Time of Occurrence." The paper outlined the study and its results. The conclusion stated that estrus-related odors are present three

Angel, a Miniature Schnauzer, sits on a platform preparing to search for cows in season among the herd. *Charlotte Schwartz*

days before estrus. The intensity of the odor rises to its peak on the day of estrus and then disappears within one day after estrus.

This definitive study opens the way for the specialized training of dogs to serve both dairy and beef herds, particularly those employing the method of artificial insemination. The small farm that maintains a bull would have little use for such dogs.

Naturally, every dog used for this type of work must be highly trained in olfactory discrimination and able to detect and discriminate scents at very low levels. In addition, the dogs must be trained to indicate their findings to their handlers.

Although research in this field is not yet complete, it is highly conceivable that the physiological changes resulting from bovine estrus can be identified by dogs from odors in the cows' manure, urine and milk in addition to the mucus.

In the years just ahead, canine olfactory researchers and dairymen will likely refine the dogs' training program and the logistics of performance to help the dairy industry cut the needless waste of labor and money and the subsequent rise in food prices of dairy products. In the future, the proverbial farm dog may be doing a lot more than just hanging around.

Buried Plastic Detection and Indication by Canines

Can you find a needle in a haystack? I can't, but my dog can. Several years ago, this dialogue would have been termed silly, ridiculous, absurd. Today we know better. We know that, thanks to the experimental work of some pioneers in canine olfaction, dogs have an amazing ability to detect a whole hoard of various items, both living and nonliving. It now remains for us to devise various methods of training dogs to detect specific odor systems.

One successful method that I devised for the detection of buried plastic is the subject of this presentation.

In late August 1977, a gentleman asked me if I could train my dog, a Miniature Schnauzer bitch named Angel, who had earned a TD, to find buried coins. He explained that a senile family member was suspected of burying a valuable coin collection in an area near a railroad track about a year previously.

Upon further investigation, I discovered the old man probably buried them in a trash bag similar to the kind used in kitchen and yard trash disposal. At that point, I realized I'd have to train her on plastic rather than metal.

After careful consideration, I advised the gentleman that:

1. I had never trained my dog to locate buried plastic, but I was willing to spend two weeks developing and testing a training method for it.
2. There was no way of knowing if the old man had, in fact, buried the coins, and if so, precisely where.

This paper was presented by the author at the meeting of the International Canine Olfaction Symposium and was published in *Off Lead* magazine, July 1978. The Symposium was held at Pennsylvania State University, State College, Pennsylvania, May 20–21, 1978.

3. If he had buried the coins, did he leave them in the plastic bag or remove them?
4. Since the old man was senile, it was entirely possible he buried them and later moved them to another location.

All of these factors pointed to a rather dubious outcome of the project, yet I consented to work on it because, my curiosity piqued, I wanted to know how successful the dog would be at locating and indicating buried plastic. We began the next day.

The training program was two-pronged. First, I obtained an assistant and presented him with a schedule of dates, places and depths where I wanted small pieces of plastic buried. I chose fields, lawns, sandy lanes, pasture land and, finally, cindery soil along a railroad track. The schedule included burying the plastic at depths of from four to twelve inches. The dates were designed to eventually have the dog locate plastic that had been buried anywhere from two to eight days.

To prepare the plastic, I cut a large green trash bag crosswise into one and half inch strips. Then I folded the strips into six inch long sections and tied each in a knot. By using knots, it gave Angel something substantial to bite into when retrieving rather than long strips flapping in her face and dragging on the ground. Each knot weighed approximately one-quarter ounce.

The training of Angel was made easier by the fact that, just a month prior to the program, she and I had studied advanced search work in Canada under Glen Johnson, the man who pioneered the training of dogs for gas pipeline leaks and gypsy moth egg masses.

Training began at a very simple level, emphasizing the fun of finding and retrieving a known object, for her a leather glove. I made sure she was hungry before taking her out for a training session, and rewarded each retrieve with a quarter-inch slice of hot dog. We began with in-sight placement and quickly graduated to out-of-sight placement of the glove. At first, out of sight meant hiding the glove under a small pile of leaves.

From that, we moved to partial out-of-sight placement. I dug a large plug of soil out of the lawn, cut the sod in half and, as the photograph shows, placed the glove in the hole, under the sod so that only the fingertips of the glove remained above the ground.

Angel, a Miniature Schnauzer, locating a piece of plastic buried beneath the ground. The black stake marks the spot for the handler who will dig it up.
Charlotte Schwartz

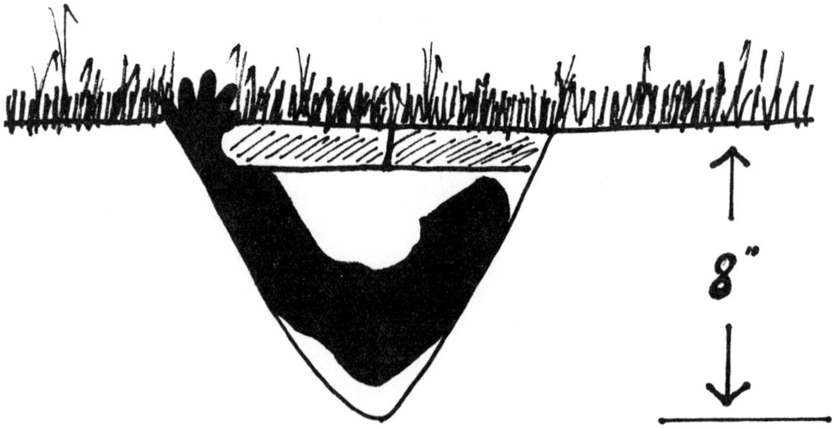

This drawing shows how a glove was buried in the lawn, covered by plugs of grass, with only the fingertips of the glove left above ground.
Charlotte Schwartz

I did not use her harness but kept her under control with a leather collar and the tracking line. It was a simple matter to encourage her to dig up the sod plug and retrieve the glove. Since she is a terrier, she is a specialist at digging and a few words of encouragement from me assured her she was doing well.

At a point midway in the two-week period, I began to wean her off the food reward, hoping to eliminate it completely during the training session and intending to feed her when we finished training each day. Then I found she was digging haphazardly and indiscriminately just to get a piece of hot dog.

Rather than taking a negative approach to the problem, I ignored the behavior and sent her after a partially buried glove and followed her find with lavish praise and food. When she dug where there was no object, I simply held back the food and praise and showed her the area of interest we were after. This worked well, and within two sessions, she realized she would have to find something before she'd get her treat.

The next step was locating an area of disturbed ground with the glove buried completely out of sight. As soon as she smelled the ground above the buried glove, she dug furiously and was praised and rewarded. At this point I began changing my verbal command from "find it," which she recognized from tracking, to "find it—seek it out."

Eventually, I dropped the "find it" and used "seek it out" exclusively. I have maintained that command to this day and found the distinction between the two has helped her understand when I expect her to track and/or search versus merely search.

Because frequently there is no track leading to the buried find due to the length of time the article had been buried, the command "seek it out" allows her more freedom and latitude in searching an area rather than looking for a track that isn't there.

Once we firmly established the find/food/praise sequence and the desired command coupled with the leather collar/line equipment, we made rapid progress toward our goal.

For the next two days, the training session (twice daily, ten minutes each) concentrated on a buried glove at various depths not aged over one hour. Each session ended with play retrieving using one of the plastic knots.

The next day we began each session with the plastic hidden under the pile of leaves. From that we worked on finding the glove which had been buried with a plastic knot, first partially covered and finally completely out of sight.

On the tenth day, Angel successfully found, and indicated by digging, plastic buried four inches under the ground an hour before. I was sure then she was actually indicating disturbed ground: I wasn't sure if she was aware of the scent of the plastic itself, and, if so, how strong was that scent. Furthermore, she had no way of telling me which was more obvious to her, the plastic or the disturbed ground. It was time to call on my assistant.

The first test came on the eleventh day of training. An alfalfa field, recently cut, was the location and the plastic had been buried hours short of two days before. As we walked up to a rise near a large buttonwood tree, I wondered if all our training was going to pay off.

Thirty feet from the tree, Angel stopped to sniff the ground. It crossed my mind then that perhaps the early morning dew might make the odor of the alfalfa stronger than that of the buried plastic. But before I could dwell on the thought, she moved another five or six feet toward the tree and began circling excitedly. Suddenly, she stopped, dug furiously and snorted as her nose filled with dirt particles. Dirt flew in a steady stream from the four inch hole she dug. Then she gave one tug and came up with the plastic knot. I grinned and my assistant shook his head as if he couldn't believe what he had seen.

Test two came that same day, about 9:00 P.M. A light drizzle was beginning to fall as Angel covered an area of our own lawn about ten feet wide by twenty feet long. My assistant held a flashlight on her and I encouraged her with "Seek it out" in an excited tone of voice. (I learned long ago one does not ever COMMAND a dog to use his nose!)

Twice she stopped and dug, but each time my assistant said, "That's not it." Each time I praised her and restarted her with a low sweep of my hand and the verbal signal to find.

The third time she stopped and began digging, my assistant smiled and I knew she was right on. This time the plastic was buried six inches down, so I held her back while our friend dug it up and gave it to her to bring to me. Food and praise followed, but all the while something bothered me. Why had she indicated two areas previous to finding the correct one? Was this the earlier problem of digging just for food rewards?

As my assistant finished replacing the dirt in the hole, I asked Angel to "Seek it out" and pointed to the areas we'd passed over. Again she began circling and twice stopped to dig.

At my request, our assistant dug up both areas. The first one yielded the blue handle of a melmac-type coffee cup, buried approximately six inches underground. It had been there more than seven years since we lived there for that length of time and never buried anything in the lawn. The second dig produced a portion of a white plastic plate, probably from the same era.

Needless to say, I was impressed with the little dog's ability, but the results of the next day's test really confused me. Test three took place about 1:00 P.M. on a very hot, dry day. The plastic was buried at a depth of six inches in the middle of a sandy lane on a nearby farm. Although Angel spent a considerable amount of time searching, she did not locate it nor did she give any indication that there was any area of interest there. The plastic had been buried for three days.

At dusk that same day, I took her to a field of pasture grass where horses graze daily. Within a minute of the time she arrived in the area, she was digging. Her find was eight inches deep and also three-days-old.

Day fourteen of the training session found us working a cindery bank alongside a railroad track. The time was late morning. There were two plastic knots buried there eight days before. She found one buried at twelve inches and the second at eight inches. She quartered well up and down the bank parallel to the tracks and found both within minutes of arrival. That night, I called my client to tell him we were ready.

We met in a town about twenty miles from my home at 9:00 A.M. on a Tuesday. Together in my car, the client, my assistant, Angel and I drove to a lonely area just outside of town and parked in the woods near the railroad track.

The two men, both carrying shovels, followed as Angel approached the bank along the track. The suspect area was originally described by the client as being approximately ten feet by fifty feet. One hour later, Angel had thoroughly covered an area fifty feet by one hundred fifty feet, with some parts of it having been double checked.

Unfortunately for the client, Angel did not find any bag containing coins. She did, however, locate and dig up a large, yellow, plastic Prestone container, a clear cleaner's bag and a small cellophane bag that had contained peanuts. All three items appeared to have been there for some period, since they showed definite signs of degradation.

Shortly after the buried plastic project, I contacted Dr. Alton Dahl, an analytical scientist at the E.I. DuPont Chemical Company in Wilmington, Delaware. I was attempting to better understand what it is that Angel is smelling when she works on plastic. I knew Dr. Dahl would have knowledge of the chemical makeup of the various items she located and perhaps that would answer some of my questions.

As for the ingredients of the various kinds of plastic and cellophane Angel located, Dr. Dahl pointed out that few were identical, although there were some similarities. As an example, polyethylene was present in several items, but not all.

The only explanation he could offer was that she was picking up the odor of trace amounts of volatile compounds arising from the degradation of the plastic articles. Therefore, we can only hypothesize that, since the volatile elements vaporize easily, the gases thus created rise to the surface through the medium in which the articles were buried and make it possible for the dog to distinguish between the odor of the soil, and biological life form therein, and the gases themselves.

It has also occurred to me that there may be a curve of ability of identification when working on buried plastics. For example, it is entirely possible that plastic buried thirty days is easier to identify than that buried five days due to the onset of degradation at the thirty-day level.

This curve may climb upward for a period of years (Dr. Dahl says it would probably be many years) and then, total degradation nearing completion, it would fall sharply to a point below that which existed shortly after the plastic was buried. Further testing over a long period of time would be required to answer these questions.

However, an interesting epilogue to this project suggests the distinct possibility of this theory.

During the two-week training period in September 1977, I buried a plastic knot between two dogwood trees, twelve inches deep in the lawn of an abandoned farmhouse. On April 11, 1978, seven months later, Angel and I were tracking at that same farm. While waiting for the track to age, I remember the buried plastic.

I put the leather collar on Angel and took her to the front lawn of the house. When she got within fifteen feet of the two trees, I gave her the verbal signal to find. By that time, her nose was already at work.

Two feet from the spot, she stopped to sniff. She circled and sniffed another spot inches from the first. Not satisfied, she continued to seek. Then she hit it. Down went the nose, the feet began tearing at the long, uncut grass and I pulled her off with much praise.

I went back to the car, got my shovel and returned with the dog to dig up the plastic exactly where she had indicated. When I removed it from the ground, I found some small roots had grown through the plastic and I preserved it as I found it.

As for the practical application of using dogs to locate and indicate buried plastic, law enforcement agencies could very likely make use of this aspect of K-9 training. My client's grandfather was not the only man who thought of burying valuables in a plastic bag! And aren't many weapons' handles made or decorated with various kinds of plastic?

Whatever the potential and the limitations of buried plastic detection by canines, I feel confident it will occupy an ever-increasing place in the curriculum of dog training.

Mandy, a Golden Retriever, leaps up to retrieve, from a tree, a packet of narcotics for owner/trainer, Kathy Uhrman. *Ken Parlini*

The Happy Hunters: Narcotics Dogs

The big engine stood like a black sentinel against the gray Colorado sky. Behind it, half a dozen freight cars sat waiting like a row of sparrows on a power line. Fifty yards down the track, a group of small buildings gathered around the station house as if they were baby chicks protecting the hen from the winds that rolled across the dusty Colorado plains.

From the station house, a tall man and a tail-wagging Golden Retriever emerged and headed for the train. The dog ran ahead of his master to greet the men working on the engine. With each greeting, the dog got a pat on the head from the workman and returned the welcome with his plumed tail wagging even more.

As the man approached, he smiled at the railroad men and greeted each with a hearty Texan, "How you doin'?"

Shortly, the dog and man left the area and headed for a car in the parking lot. At the car, a heavyset man waited to bid them farewell. "How'd it go, Carl?"

"Fine today!" exclaimed the man with the dog as they drove off. What appeared to be a casual visit was instead a very thorough inspection for narcotics by an extremely sensitive dog who knew exactly what he was looking for.

His master is Carl Rickert, former New Hampshire and Texas State Trooper, now owner of BJR Security Service, a large detective agency in Gainesville, Texas. The dog, Drummer, is a narcotics dog.

The illegal sale of narcotics is the second biggest money-making business in the United States. And it's much more than that. It is responsible for on-the-job injuries, absenteeism, crime and loss of valuable man-hours.

Today businesses such as major railroads, industries and

local government agencies are using narcotics dogs to cut down on the use of drugs in and around work areas by employees.

Later that same day in a school in Gainesville, Texas, Drummer moved slowly down a long hall lined with students' lockers. Again, it appeared almost a casual walk, but this time Drummer was searching for narcotics stashed inside those lockers.

By now, Drummer was a familiar sight in the halls of the schools in the Dallas/Fort Worth area. The children knew exactly what his mission was: To find and indicate narcotics brought into the school by the students.

They also knew that, should something happen to Drummer, there was another Golden Retriever, Rebel, waiting to take his place. The word was getting around that school was no place to hide drugs, and the school was becoming quite free of them thanks to Drummer and Rickert.

On a small island in New York Harbor, another Golden Retriever goes about her business of using her nose to protect one of America's most treasured landmarks. The dog's name is Talli and she lives and works on Liberty Island.

Like a goddess rising up out of the fog, the Statue of Liberty stands tall and serene as the morning mist evaporates around her. At the dock, a ferryboat chugs alongside to unload its cargo of tourists who have come to see the great lady.

Many are there because their ancestors, perhaps even some themselves, saw the statue for the first time from the deck of a ship bringing them, as immigrants, to these shores from another country. This day, however, they have come to see her from within.

Talli's job is to make sure their visit will be a safe one, free from bombs and explosives surreptitiously planted on the island by terrorists.

As the tourists begin debarking, Talli sits patiently waiting to greet her guests, the ever-wagging golden tail announcing her pleasure at seeing them. Small children stop to pet her as her handler stands smiling beside her. Occasionally a lady will bend over to pet Talli on the head and mutter some endearing words, never suspecting that her own safety is being assured by the friendly dog.

As the tourists begin to move away, Talli strolls off with

her handler to patrol the island. Occasionally the man will stop and let her run free to break up the pace. From his pocket he takes a canvas bag, about the size of a man's leather glove, and tosses it for Talli to fetch. Inside the bag is a small amount of gun powder that serves to remind her of the scent she must be constantly searching for. If, however, she finds an explosive, she will not be allowed to retrieve it for safety purposes. But this bag is hers, this game is theirs, and she cherishes them both.

Dogs that search for bombs and narcotics are among the largest growing group of canine olfactory specialists in the world. They are being trained to sniff out heroin, marijuana, cocaine, methaqualone, and many other lesser known narcotics.

The dogs indicate their finds in a variety of ways. Some sit or stand quietly. Others bark and dig furiously at the spot where the find is made. Still others lie down beside it and simply stare intently, first at the spot and then at the handler.

Each dog is trained individually for a specific job in a specific environment. For example, Talli was trained to find explosives and she wouldn't recognize a marijuana cigarette if she saw one. But let someone plant a bomg or other explosive on Liberty Island and she'll locate it in minutes! Indoors, Talli can find an explosive in ten seconds in a small room. Outdoors, it takes a little longer.

Compare that time to the amount of time it would take a man to locate the same package and you quickly realize how efficient bomb and narcotics dogs are to have around. Add to that the fact that the olfactory ability of a dog is between one thousand and ten thousand times greater than man's and you have some pretty impressive statistics.

When you compare one man's wages per hour against the cost of training and maintaining a scent dog, it's easy to understand why scent dogs are more in demand than ever before.

The cost of producing a trained bomb or narcotics dog is approximately $2,500. This includes the cost of the dog itself, ten weeks of training plus room and board for the entire ten weeks for the dog and the final week's room and board and transportation for the handler. In other words, a good scent dog is usually valued at about $5,000. People familiar with the track record of these dogs admit their value is far above the cost.

Dog and handler searching for marijuana. (Note vent along side window.)

Captain Haggerty's School for Dogs

Dog retraces his steps along building in search of marijuana. *Captain Haggerty's School for Dogs*

Dog locates marijuana inside vent.

Captain Haggerty's School for Dogs

The people who teach scent dogs to do what they do are as different as the dogs themselves, yet in many ways they are very like the dogs they teach. If that sounds a bit contradictory, let's take a closer look at the dogs and their teachers.

Everyone recognizes the fact that all Golden Retrievers, for example, look very similar just as do all German Shepherd Dogs, all Cocker Spaniels and all Beagles. However, if one has ever known two of any one breed, one quickly becomes aware that each dog within a given breed is unique in many ways, such as temperament, personality, etc.

So then are the people who train dogs. Some, for example, are outgoing, some retiring and quiet. Some are very physical, while others take a more intellectual approach to training.

In other words, one can find dog trainers among many types of personalities, and they can all be excellent at doing what they do. Each can tailor his training style to suit his or her own unique personality while keeping the criteria the same for the product they produce. Consequently, you can have two Golden Retrievers that look alike trained by two men who look alike, each dog trained in a different manner yet whose performance on the job is similar.

There are, however, certain characteristics of the dogs who succeed at this type of work that are similar to corresponding characteristics in the humans who teach them. Enthusiasm for learning is a prime example. The dogs must be willing workers, eager to learn from their human companions, capable of paying attention to their trainers and keeping their minds on the task at hand. The trainers, too, must be enthusiastic about what they're teaching, eager to work with dogs and capable of concentrating on successfully teaching each small step before moving on to the next.

In addition, both dogs and humans must have the capacity to be patient with the other and possess a drive to success that far outweighs the total frustration of occasional failures and problems. They must be able to bounce back with enthusiasm regardless of the number of times they come upon small stumbling blocks.

These are the marks of the teams who will make it. Some will take longer than others, but the time factor isn't nearly as important as the degree of success they achieve because, in the

Kathy Uhrman training a Golden Retriever to locate narcotics in a locker.
Ken Parlini

Mandy finds narcotics hidden under the bumper of a van.
Ken Parlini

end, the dogs must love what they do and do it one hundred percent of the time. There is no room for failure when a bomb is in the picture.

Let's examine the team of Kathy Uhrman and Dawn. Kathy appears to the casual onlooker as a young, middle-class American wife with a lovely home in the New Jersey suburbs, a small daughter and a busy schedule of activities ranging from carpooling children to school to socializing with her executive husband.

Her chestnut hair is neatly braided and pinned on top of her head for daytime activities and let down at social events. Her dress is blue jeans around the house and blue satin at parties. She's a bubbly, pleasant person, very interested in what others have to say, yet equally at ease explaining how she grows the flowers in her garden. Like so many young housewives today, she drives a big van and shops for bargains at the supermarket.

When visitors come to the Uhrman home, they barely pull into the long winding driveway when out comes the owner to greet them. This, however, is where the similarity to other homemakers ends. For as she approaches the visitors, Kathy is skirted by five happy Golden Retrievers circling her, barking, tails wagging as if they were attached to her blue jeans. She wears the dogs well and, after a moment, turns to them and says in a not-very-genteel voice, "OK! That's enough. Quiet!"

The dogs immediately stop barking and run over to investigate the visitors. One of them, Dawn, picks up a stick lying in the grass and brings it like a peace offering to the guests, her golden plume fanning the air.

Behind the Uhrman home there is a large building used as a kennel with chain-link runs jutting out from the long side facing the house. Kathy Uhrman keeps twenty Golden Retrievers there, all of whom are either shown in the breed ring, used for breeding or being trained as bomb and narcotics dogs.

The bomb dogs also greet every visitor with the same happy Golden Retriever "Hi! I'm so glad to see ya!" style of welcome. It is exactly this warm, loving personality that makes Kathy Uhrman's dogs so valuable for narcotics work.

Bomb and narcotic dogs work amidst people. They work in all types of public places, such as train and bus stations, restaurants and high schools. The people who handle these dogs need friendly canines who will not frighten or intimidate adults and children. Thus, the Golden Retriever, with its friendly manner and happy attitude, is ideal for the job.

Uhrman begins training a bomb and narcotics dog by playing fetch-the-towel with the dog. As soon as she's sure the dog has an insatiable appetite for retrieving, she switches from the towel to a canvas bag filled with gunpowder. Once the dog gets used to the scent of the powder, she begins playing a hide-and-seek game with the bag. In her happy, exuberant style, she encourages the dog to find the bag, first under a pile of leaves perhaps, then progressing to more difficult locations.

Always the dog is made to feel the training is a game and he wants to play. Each time the dog is successful, Kathy and the dog stop and celebrate with petting, praise and lots of excitement. If she is training the dog for narcotics, she fills the bag with marijuana and proceeds to other drugs as the dog develops proficiency at each.

Kathy Uhrman is one of the few women civilians in the United States (she was the first back in 1980) to hold a federal license from the United States Drug Enforcement Administration to possess all narcotics for training dogs.

Following the filing of a lengthy application and a subsequent investigation into her background, she is now able to purchase narcotics from pharmacies. Usually she trains the dogs to find the more widely used drugs such as heroin, marijuana, cocaine and methaqualone.

Her dogs have been sold to private individuals and law enforcement agencies around the country. Rebel and Drummer, for example, went to Private Detective Richert in Texas where they work around railroads and in public schools. The Paterson, New Jersey, Police Department owns one of her dogs, Misty, who joined the police force before she was a year old. Within two years, Misty had made more than twenty busts.

A private detective on Long Island, New York, owns one of the Uhrman Goldens, and the Sheriff's Department in West Palm Beach, Florida, has ordered two bomb dogs for now and wants more in the near future.

Uhrman's dog, Talli, is the bomb dog guarding the Statue of Liberty. Actually, she got started in scent work training in 1981 when she donated Talli to the United States Park Service. Talli

A Golden Retriever locates a packet of cocaine secured to the underside of a train. *Ken Parlini*

Even the platform of a caboose can make an ideal place for hiding drugs, but the Golden Retriever will find it despite man's efforts to hide it. *Ken Parlini*

went to Fayetteville, North Carolina, to be trained for the job on Liberty Island by Gerry Lapham of Sentinel K-9 School there.

Keeping abreast of Talli's progress, Uhrman became fascinated by the dog's olfactory ability. She decided to take some Goldens to Lapham and study training herself. Since then, she and Lapham have trained many bomb and narcotics dogs together and travel between North Carolina and New Jersey several times a year. With each dog working approximately ten weeks in the training process, it appears Kathy Uhrman will have a waiting list for a long time to come.

The final two weeks bring the new handlers to study under the trainer so they can handle the dog once its training is complete. Both Uhrman and Lapham insist that this transition period be accomplished under the watchful eye of the trainer so the dog maintains its enthusiasm and accuracy of performance on the job site.

It is essential that extreme caution be exercised in making the transition from trainer to final handler. Handled improperly, the dog would burn out and stop working with little hope of rehabilitation to another handler on another job site. In the case of Talli there are two handlers and both men had to spend the last two weeks of Talli's training working with her in North Carolina.

Private individuals are not the only ones training scenting dogs. Many law enforcement agencies and government bureaus train similar dogs. The United States Army, for example, has trained hundreds of narcotics and bomb dogs at the Aberdeen Proving Grounds in Maryland. The United States Customs Service trains their dogs in Front Royal, Virginia.

Many cities and states also have their own canine corps trained in locating bombs, narcotics, lost persons and escaped felons. The Philadelphia, Pennsylvania, Police Department Canine Corps has its own school and instructors and is rated one of the best in the country. In New York State, police canines are trained at the State Police Academy in Albany where, in November 1982, they graduated seven German Shepherd Dogs into the force.

In assessing the future of bomb and narcotics dogs, Kathy Uhrman said, "Number one, we've got to get drugs out of our schools. And the dogs can do it quickly, easily, and peacefully. As for bomb dogs, the United States has been lucky to escape terrorism so far, but it's coming. Look what happened in England in 1982. Bomb dogs can prevent the same thing from happening here."

Whether guarding against explosives at one of America's most historical sites, searching for marijuana in school lockers or cocaine being smuggled into the country through one of our airports, harbors or border crossings, dogs are making a significant contribution to maintaining the quality of life for all Americans. The most intriguing quality of the scent dogs themselves is that man will never know exactly how they do it.

A tracking dog leads its handler along a path of a person who has gone ahead of them minutes or hours before. *Charlotte Schwartz*

Canine Olfactory Specialists

The gently undulating terrain rolled on ahead of them for miles with an occasional road crossing the fields and disappearing over the horizon. The Canadian sun began to rise and burn off the haze of the night to reveal a farmer already plowing his field. In the distance, like two tiny ants climbing the hills and valleys of a footprint, the man and his dog moved across the land.

The dog, a dark and handsome German Shepherd Dog named Sam, would run ahead of his master, sniff the ground, then stop and look back impatiently at the man. As his owner approached, the Shepherd would once again put his nose to the ground and swirl away to move out ahead, all the while acting the part of a gamboling pup yet an athlete whose every muscle rippled under the sleek black and tan coat giving hint that this dog was more than a gentle giant. To the untrained eye, the scene was of a big dog out for a stroll and enjoying every minute of it.

The man, tall, medium weight and sandy-haired, walked briskly on long legs that covered the ground efficiently. He wore a khaki jacket, an old hat to keep the morning mist from his head and well-worn boots that had carried him through all manner of terrain for many miles before this day.

As the dog romped ahead, the man watched the animal with an intensity that said this was more than just a morning stroll. Periodically, he would call ahead to the dog and offer encouragement.

"Where is it?" he'd ask the dog. The animal would put his nose to the ground again and continue his search despite the hum of the plowing tractor moving toward them.

Suddenly, the dog stopped, sniffed hard at the rich, brown

soil and began digging at it with both paws. The soil flew beneath his tensed body as his nose dropped ever lower into the dirt.

The man came running over to join the dog. "Good boy! Good boy!" exclaimed his owner as he patted the dog in celebration.

For here, in this Canadian field with the sun getting serious about starting the day and the wind picking up from the West, history was being made. But, like so many pioneers before them, there were no crowds to cheer them on, no television or radio announcers to shout to the world what the dog had just accomplished.

There were only a few other dog handlers, a Canadian gas company official and the farmer to witness the first occasion when a dog successfully found a gas leak from a pipeline buried beneath the ground.

The year was 1975, the dog was a canine olfactory specialist and the man was his owner, trainer and best friend.

The story of dogs that locate gas leaks in underground pipelines, gypsy moth egg masses in the forest and dielectric fluid leaks beneath blacktop and cement is the story of one man: Glen Johnson. A Canadian, Johnson is an electronics teacher at St. Clair College in Windsor, Ontario, and runs a popular dog obedience training school in the evenings. In addition, Johnson is founder and director of the Windsor Police Department Canine Corps.

Weekends and summers, Johnson teaches tracking training to people and their dogs. In addition, he gives lectures and seminars across the United States and Canada. And, in 1975, he wrote the book, *Tracking Dog: Training and Methods* (Arner Publications), that has become the training bible for thousands of dogs and their owners.

The unique aspect of the man is the scent work he has done with his own dogs, all German Shepherds, in order to help mankind achieve nearly impossible goals in locating solids, liquids and gases that cannot be seen with the naked eye nor detected by sophisticated monitoring devices. In his most recent endeavor, he did it in the middle of New York City traffic!

His first such project began in 1975 when a firm that had designed a natural gas pipeline in Canada contracted with him

Glen Johnson and an observer watching a dog track. *Charlotte Schwartz*

Glen Johnson gives instructions to a track layer. *Charlotte Schwartz*

to train handlers and dogs to locate and indicate to those handlers leaking butyl mercaptan along a 94-mile stretch of land from Windsor to Sarnia. The pipeline was buried beneath the ground and monitoring devices had shown leaks, but the leak detection equipment had failed to indicate their location.

Dogs were the obvious choice for this job since they had previously proven their olfactory proficiency in such areas as animal and man tracking and in detecting drugs, firearms and explosives. Their sensitivity to minute particles of a wide variety of odor systems and their willingness to work closely with man made them ideal candidates for this project. German Shepherd Dogs were used because Sam and the two other Shepherds were already trained, experienced trackers.

Since the underlying motive for tracking dogs is the desire to find and retrieve, specialized scent detection work should begin with dogs that are successful trackers. Johnson uses a method he had devised earlier for obedience training which he calls the Inducive Retrieve Method.

Simply put, the method rewards the dog for retrieving and offers total indifference when the dog does not retrieve. Dogs, being social animals and wanting to please their human partners, quickly learn the value of positive behavior and are eager to find and retrieve without harsh or abusive training methods. The effects of this type of training produce happy, reliable performances in the shortest amount of time.

Once Johnson had selected the two other handlers and dogs that would work with him on the gas pipeline project, it took less than three days to train the dogs on a simulated buried pipeline at the edge of a parking lot in Windsor, Ontario. Next, on the actual job site, the handlers and dogs worked for nine days searching for the real gas leaks. At the end of that time, the score was more than 150 leaks, some close to the surface, others eighteen inches below it, under roadways and freshly plowed fields, all of which had been missed by the leak detection equipment! A truly amazing feat and one that launched new horizons for dogs and man in the area of olfactory work.

United States Customs Service Detector Dogs

The big jet glides into the landing zone, burning rubber as giant tires skim cement. The veteran pilot brings the airship to a halt in front of a concourse filled with excited people waiting to greet loved ones, business associates and friends. But there will be more waiting yet. Unloading baggage and customs inspection is next.

. . . .

In the United States Customs Service area, passengers and baggage will be carefully scrutinized to determine that no one carries narcotics, dangerous drugs, hidden weapons or explosives into the country. Therein lies the story of the United States Customs Service Canine Enforcement Program. A story filled with mystery, intrigue and wonder.

We can read about the mystery and intrigue in any large newspaper every day of the week. But the wonder part is the almost unbelievable job performed by the Customs dogs as they go about their business of detecting illegal goods being smuggled across our borders. And they do it with nothing more than a pair of good nostrils, the desire to please their handlers and a will to work.

Detector dogs were originally introduced in the Customs Service in September 1970 to help officials cut down on the importation of illegal goods. They are used at international airports, seaports and border crossings.

German Shepherd Dogs, Labrador Retrievers, Golden Retrievers, Brittanies, German Shorthaired Pointers and mixed breeds are among the most used. Virtually all of the large working dogs and sporting dogs plus large mixed breeds are considered for the job.

Breed alone is not the only consideration for selection as a Customs dog. Dogs must pass a battery of tests to determine temperament, sociability and trainability. They must be physically sound, of either sex, between one and three years of age and possess a strong desire to retrieve. Only about one in every forty-five dogs passes the tests.

They should have some obedience training and be extremely self-confident because their work will take them into many situations where self-reliance will be essential. They may be working an airport baggage room one day and climbing through freight cars on a railroad siding the next. They must board ships, airplanes, mail trucks, big sea-going containers and passenger cars.

They work the hot desert, misty harbors, frigid Northwest and any other place a Customs canine team is required. They examine hundreds of pieces of luggage a day, search thousands of pieces of mail and their noses must never fail them. In short, they must possess all-area capabilities.

In 1981 alone Customs canine teams seized over $189 million worth of narcotics and dangerous drugs in a total of 4,522 finds. They found 35,780 pounds of marijuana, 308 pounds of cocaine, 57 pounds of heroin, 15,190 pounds of hashish, 2 pounds of morphine and opium and 2,094,524 dangerous drug units. Compared to budget dollars spent, that's a 62 to 1 return in terms of drug street value.

One good detector dog can rack up a significant record of seizures in a very short time. Scorpio is an excellent example of this. A black Labrador Retriever, Scorpio has been stationed in Miami since 1976.

During his years of service there he has made a total of 433 seizures. The largest single find was 286 pounds of cocaine. Among his other credits is locating a total of 31,974 pounds of marijuana and 45,371 units of dangerous drugs. With a record like this, Scorpio is likely to become one of the all-time super scenters in the Customs Service.

Where does the Customs Service obtain these super scenters? The dogs are acquired from a variety of sources. Animal shelters provide some. Individual owners donate a large percentage of the dogs and the Service occasionally purchases some.

Once a dog makes it through all the tests with a passing score, he begins his training at the Canine Enforcement Training Center in Front Royal, Virginia. There he will be assigned a handler and, together, they will go through fourteen weeks of intensive training. He will begin by learning to play tug-of-war with an old towel. Eventually, he will find himself playing with a pouch made of toweling and filled wih one of the major drugs or narcotics.

The next step finds the handler hiding the favorite pouch in a variety of places and encouraging the dog to "Find it!" As the training progresses to more serious matters, the handler and dog build a bond between them that will ultimately carry them through the toughest assignment.

Eventually the dog will respond to all narcotics and many amphetamines and barbiturates due to the similarities in processing. If the dog is going to be used to locate and indicate weapons and explosives, his training will be geared toward the scent of the components of explosives.

During his training and career, the dog will live in a comfortable kennel owned by the Customs Service or in a boarding kennel hired by them. In addition to his regular assignment, the dog has to be readily available to answer special duty calls from state, local and foreign law enforcement agencies as well as the United States Coast Guard.

Handlers of these dogs come from the Civil Service or other departments of the Customs Service itself. While in training, they actually train two dogs simultaneously. One dog will eventually become the handler's full-time partner and the other dog will replace a dog being retired from the Service.

One such handler is a man named Charles Caldwell, a forty-five-year-old father of four children ranging in age from sixteen to twenty-two. Although Caldwell is now an instructor and course developer, he served in the field for many years. He has teamed with a German Shepherd Dog, a mixed breed and currently handles a Labrador Retriever on special duty assignments.

A veteran of the United States Air Force, Caldwell has served in almost every capacity within the Customs Service Canine Enforcement Program from kennel master to his present instructor status. As a young Air Force man he worked

Charles Caldwell and partner, a German Shepherd Dog.
United States Customs Service

in the Security Police and canine programs. For the Customs Service, he has instructed both the Sentry Dog and Narcotics Dog Programs.

The Customs Service employs men and women and currently has two women handlers in the canine program. Sex is not a determining factor in the choice of handlers. It is a simple fact that there are certain individuals, both men and women, who have the intelligence, stamina and agility to work with the dogs. Perhaps the most important factor, however, is the intangible quality of naturalness required to work dogs that makes for a successful canine detector team.

Like Caldwell, every handler wants to stop the flow of narcotics and dangerous drugs coming into the country. As Caldwell says, "By this means, we are attempting to cut back on narcotic-related crimes in the United States."

How many dogs are in the service at any one time? "The number of dogs in service is determined by the threat analysis at all airports, seaports and land border crossings," answers Caldwell. That means the Front Royal Training Center must train approximately forty to fifty dogs per year to maintain enough canine scent specialists to cover America's 22,000 miles of borders.

As *America the Beautiful* says, we are a land of spacious skies from sea to shining sea. The handlers and dogs of the United States Customs Service are dedicated to protecting that land and the quality of the lives within it.

Deer Search Dogs

Somewhere deep within the soul of most men lies a principle of decency that demands that man, as a predator, must not allow his prey to die as a result of prolonged suffering. His death blow shall be swift and sure, and the prey must drop on the spot.

Dr. John Jeanneney, Professor of History at Hofstra University on Long Island, New York, and an avid deer hunter, is committed to helping his fellow hunters realize that principle. And his little wirehaired Dachshund, Clary, makes it all possible.

Back in 1972, Jeanneney had been deer hunting on Long Island when he sighted and shot a deer only to have it get away. After many miles and a whole day's search, he finally gave up, knowing he had wounded but not killed his prey. He went home that night with a heavy heart and a pledge to do something about never letting it happen again.

Not long after that incident, Jeanneney applied to the New York State Department of Environmental Conservation for a special research permit that would allow him to use leashed tracking dogs to locate wounded deer. Once found, the deer could be quickly destroyed to cut short their suffering and, at the same time, save good venison.

The use of dogs in hunting is as old as the man-dog relationship itself. For the early men who practiced it, it provided food, clothing, and the makings of tool parts and utensils.

It wasn't until modern times that sports hunters appeared on the scene. They were the ones who went hunting for the simple pleasure of having a bearskin rug or a deer head to hang on the wall. When sports hunters emerged, other men felt the need to design controls against the mass killing of some of the world's greatest mammals.

Consequently, hunting big game such as deer and bear with dogs is illegal in most states, although there are some in the southern part of the United States that still permit it. Those states do so because they have particularly rough and impenetrable terrain and they want to prevent the game from starving to death due to overpopulation.

Many states, however, permit the use of dogs in hunting small game such as squirrel, rabbit, raccoon and fox for the same reason.

Jeanneney had learned firsthand about the German method of hunting wounded animals by tracking their blood trails. In France, where he studied as a Fulbright scholar at the French National Forestry School, he met German students who told him of the work of Dachshunds in their country and Austria.

Dachshunds, he learned, originated in Germany where they were and still are used for blood tracking as well as for hunting badger and fox. Their hard coat and strong legs make them particularly suitable for this type of work. Since the dogs work on leash, they never have the opportunity to chase healthy deer.

Once Jeanneney obtained the research permit, he began teaching his little Clary how to follow the blood trails of wounded deer. Combining the methods used in Germany and assisted by a French wildlife manager-friend, he soon had the dog working a blood trail at least twenty-four hours old and several miles long through scrub, brush, meadows and streams.

For the next four years, Jeanneney and Clary worked wounded deer trails alone while the dog scored better than twenty finds, all of which were quickly dispatched to end their suffering. As the little Dachshund's record grew more impressive, Jeanneny began hoping he could convince New York State authorities that it was, indeed, feasible to license blood trailing dogs that could be used on a regular basis by deer hunters.

There were no accurate figures on how many deer are wounded yet not killed annually, but from his own hunting experiences Jeanneney knew the number was probably staggering.

In 1977, an incident occurred that brought Jeanneney's work out into the open and ultimately led to the birth of Deer

Clary, a Deer Search Dachshund, led owner, John Jeanneney, and hunter to the location of this fallen deer. *unknown*

Clary gets a hug from owner, John Jeanneney, after locating a fallen buck deer. *unknown*

Search, Inc. It was January and New York State had announced a special deer hunting season on Long Island. The hunt was initiated to cut down the deer population so the survivors would not die from starvation.

A hunter by the name of Frank Deos had shot an eight point buck late in the day. Deos had seen the deer hit and watched helplessly as the wounded animal raced deep into the woods. As the light of the day turned to winter grey and finally dark, the hunter realized he'd have to give up the search and go home. It bothered him that, although he'd seen the shot hit the deer and some blood fall to the dried leaves of the forest floor, he was unable to locate the animal and end its suffering.

Back home, Deos related the sad story to a friend who was a state biologist. The biologist urged him to call on Jeanneney and Clary for help.

Four hours later, Jeanneney and Clary picked up the trail where the buck's blood had fallen to the ground at the spot where it had been shot. A quarter of a mile later, Clary, leaning hard into her harness, led the men to the buck, still alive but in shock. The hunter finished his job quickly.

Two more years passed before Jeanneney founded Deer Search, Inc., with two other hunter-dog owner friends, Don Hickman and Hans Klein. They designed the organization to address two goals. First, it would provide basic information on deer anatomy to hunters. With this knowledge the hunters could minimize wounding the deer and increase the number of quick kills. Second, it would provide leashed tracking dogs to locate wounded deer as a final solution when hunters lose the trail of wounded deer. In addition, the organization developed a program of slide presentations aimed at educating hunters and other interested groups.

More dogs were imported from Germany and trained. The men tried other breeds of dogs. A German Shorthaired Pointer and a German Wirehaired Pointer proved successful. They developed tests for the dogs and handlers. They kept in touch with their German advisors and solved each training and testing problem as it arose.

Operational funds came out of their own pockets and even today none of them ever receives pay for the time they spend training or searching. Knowing they have shared their love and concern for wildlife is the only reward they have ever received.

As Jeanneney says, "I was motivated to see that what happened to me did not happen to other hunters."

Finally, in 1981, New York State Assemblyman Glen Warren and State Senator Jay Rolison introduced a bill that could authorize the licensed use of leashed tracking dogs for locating wounded big game. The bill requires handlers to serve an apprenticeship, pass a test and a review of their own hunting history.

As for the dogs, their test is based on the German standards. A dog must find a fresh frozen deerskin at the end of a half-mile trail laid with only a half pint of blood at least twenty-four hours before.

Today Deer Search, Inc., operates in Suffolk and Dutchess Counties with a total of eight handlers and dogs. In the seven years since Jeanneney began, he and his fellow members have found a total of ninety wounded deer, with the individual dog's record being claimed by Clary.

Now eleven years old, Clary has found more than sixty deer and she's still tracking. In the future, she will act as a back-up for some of the younger dogs and serve as a leader in the most difficult searches. Her ability to track wounded deer has surely helped hunters to uphold one of mankind's basic principles of decency.

PART IV

Dogs in the Future

Dogs in the Future

Where will the man/dog relationship be fifty years from now? If mankind seizes the opportunities offered by the current renaissance in his relationship with dogs, it is conceivable that life will not only be assured for both species, but could become richer.

Take, for instance, a dog trained to detect a specific odor system. Man's use of that dog's olfactory ability can save him money, time and effort. It could earn him fame. It could bring him wealth. It could lead to new horizons in mastering what he himself can never know, that little understood skill of olfactory sensitivity that his canine partner possesses yet cannot recount to him.

The dog, on the other hand, could find meaningful activity rather than laze away his life in mere existence. He could receive much sought-after attention from his human pack members. And, finally, he could develop a rewarding relationship with his master.

Most importantly, mankind can be the benefactor of yet unimagined achievements that will improve the quality of his life.

Although the use of dogs in this symbiotic relationship is limited only by man's imagination, some of the jobs that may be forthcoming in the future are listed here for consideration by those who may be interested in trying out new concepts.

Sign Language Dogs for the Deaf. Many hearing-impaired people never learn to speak because they cannot hear the spoken word. It would seem feasible then that dogs could be trained to read Ameslan, American sign language. With the canine sensitivity to the slightest movement, it would not be difficult to teach this skill and it would most likely offer the opportunity of ownership to people who would otherwise never think they could own a dog.

Espionage Equipment Detector Dogs. In his book, *New Techniques in Canine Training and Development,* author Captain G. L. Hulse, R.A.E. (The Wentworth Press, Australia) mentions the future possibilities of dogs detecting mines, booby traps and similar man-made devices. It also seems possible that dogs could be trained to reconnoiter, locate concealed weapons caches and warn of advancing enemy troops. With the sophistication of today's electronic equipment, dogs could be trained to respond to electronic commands so they can perform tasks far away from human handlers.

Water Leak Dogs. Here's another olfactory behavior of dogs that is probably just around the corner. Locating water leaks deep underground where monitoring devices cannot detect them is a likely job for dogs in the near future. With their highly sensitive noses, the dogs' scenting ability would not be affected by macadam and concrete surfaces.

Chemicals and Precious Metal Dogs. The efficiency of Geiger counters and other similar instruments could be augmented by these detector dogs. When the decision to dig lay in the balance, dogs could be used to help make that final choice.

Fingerprint Dogs. This is a fascinating area that law enforcement agencies are bound to discover for a man's scent is as distinct a trait as his fingerprints to dogs. It takes police officers many hours to search a location for fingerprints in crime cases. Using dogs to first imprint the scent of a suspect then locate that same scent on objects in a room or vehicle could save time and money. The dog's findings could then be substantiated by regular fingerprint procedures. This training could also make stolen articles easily identifiable.

Insect Detection Dogs. Glen Johnson has already trained dogs to locate and indicate gypsy moth egg masses. Several people have trained dogs to do the same with termites. But think of the thousands of kinds of insects in the world and how helpful it would be to have dogs trained for the early detection of some of mankind's most bothersome or dangerous pests.

Smoke Detector Dogs. Douglas Kirk, an animal psychologist from Texas, trained two mixed breed dogs to detect smoke in an apartment and, using nose-pushing responses, indicate their findings to a machine monitor. The project did not culminate in long-term reliability, however. The dogs, it seemed, just wouldn't work for the machine even though it produced food at every correct response.

In the future, it is entirely feasible that this type of work could be developed to produce the desired results. It is also likely that, since dogs are social animals and require leadership from a pack member, they will periodically need some form of interaction with humans.

Truffles Dogs. Pigs search for truffles, a mushroom-type delicacy, in France. Now dogs are being trained to do the same in the United States.

Labrador Retrievers are quite successful at finding the truffles growing beneath the surface of the soil in Texas. Due to the high cost of truffles, it appears the man who has a truffles-detecting dog may have more than just a pet in his dog.

Alcoholic Rehabilitation Dogs. Dogs have already been found useful in helping to rehabilitate alcoholics in Connecticut, Colorado and Illinois. From these meager beginnings, hospitals and institutions will undoubtedly expand the use of dogs to help alcoholic patients renew their interest in life and find a purpose in useful activities and interactions with their fellow man.

These are but the tip of the man/dog iceberg. The real future of the dog's role in improving the quality of life for mankind is what lies beneath the surface in man's own imagination.

Perhaps the best definition of the present renaissance in the man/dog relationship was expressed recently by a scientist when he said, "It is the living together in intimate association of two dissimilar organisms to the advantage of both." Heady words, for sure, but they say it all. Together, we can make it. Individually we may not.

Dr. Konrad Lorenz, Nobel Prize winning ethologist.

Future Research Paths

The International Symposium on the Human/Pet Relationship

They came from all over the world. More than 300 people from 180 countries on five continents. They came to listen, learn, share and compare. Only the subject of their gathering was of universal interest.

The occasion was the International Symposium on the Human/Pet Relationship honoring the eightieth birthday of Nobel Prize winner Dr. Konrad Lorenz. The Symposium was held on October 27–28, 1983 in Vienna, Austria, at the Austrian Academy of Sciences.

Vienna. A city out of the pages of a history book. Vienna, with its Romanesque and Gothic cathedrals and palaces. Vienna, where the Blue Danube meanders through the countryside and St. Stephen's Plaza is the hub of modern, sophisticated people in a picturesque Renaissance setting.

During the two days a variety of experts from both Western and Eastern European countries, Australia and the United States presented papers on the latest scientific findings in the field of man/animal relations. The subjects they covered were as varied as the countries from which they came.

Dr. Lorenz addressed the congress and thrilled the audience with his simple, yet profound, words of wisdom for which he has become famous. A genetic theoretician, Lorenz was the first scientist to address his teachings to the common man rather than limiting his findings to other scientists. He spoke of man's relationship to other animals and how they all interact with their environment. And he warned of the consequences of ignoring these facts.

"Today," he said, "we see dangerous changes in man, a shift in reality, so to speak. The great danger lies in the fact that man accepts as reality only those things which he can see and quantify and feel. Therefore, technological matters and money become so important.

"It is a simple fact that you cannot spend more than you earn. People simply refuse to accept this and one day man will create conditions where sunlight is no longer available in sufficient amounts and this will lead the world to disaster.

"Man has lost his belief that reality is more than things you can see and feel and count. And this social epidemic will lead the world to catastrophe simply because we go along expending ourselves.

"That's why the interdisciplinary studies of man/animal are of such extreme importance. Man is not an autonomous creature. He lives in this world as an open system in association with other open systems and there must be a balance between man, animals and nature for us all to survive."

Since 1963 Lorenz has written more than two dozen books devoted to the subject of man, animals and ethology. *Man Meets Dog, The Year of the Graylag Goose* and *King Solomon's Ring* are among his many publications which have been printed in English. In addition, Lorenz is a Professor at the Austrian Academy of Sciences where he heads the research department of ethology.

During the two-day Symposium, a variety of fascinating subjects were addressed. "Pet Population and the Pet/Owner Bond," "Pet Therapy," "A Dog in Residence in a Geriatric Hospital in Australia," "The Communication Systems Between Children and Dogs," "The Influence of Petkeeping on Social Competence in Children" and "Companion Animals in Foster Homes" were just some of the subjects covered.

More general subjects such as petkeeping in zoological gardens, physiological and behavioral responses to interaction with companion animals, a comparison of urban versus rural petkeeping and the biological aspects of behavior of man/animal relations were presented.

Among the speakers there were many well-known experts from the United States: Drs. Alan Beck and Aaron Katcher, University of Pennsylvania; Dr. Michael McCulloch, Portland, Oregon; Dr. Leo Bustad, Washington State University; Dr. Dan

Lago, Pennsylvania State University; Dr. Stephen Kellert, Yale University; Dr. Eckhard Hess, University of Chicago. Their talks covered a broad range of subjects within the discipline of the man/animal bond. All stressed that this relatively new science needs worldwide recognition and understanding.

Interest in the bond began in the 1960s when Dr. Boris Levinson, a New York psychiatrist, found that the presence of a pet during psychiatric sessions greatly facilitated contact with his patients, particularly those who were uncommunicative. Levinson also wrote of the potential emotional and educational benefits of pet ownership for normal children.

The Lorenz Symposium was the latest in a series of meetings on the bond. The first was in London in 1974. Then, in 1979, a small group of interested people met in Dundee, Scotland. From that meeting the Society for Companion Animal Studies was founded.

There were two major international conferences on the bond prior to the Lorenz Symposium. The first was held in London, England, in 1980; the second in Philadelphia, Pennsylvania, in 1981 to which over 300 delegates attended. Perhaps the most significant contribution of the Lorenz Symposium was the blending of findings and opinions from the research, educational and practical aspects of the bond.

For example, Jim Eve, from Australia, spoke on the therapeutic value of keeping a resident dog, in this case a yellow Labrador Retriever by the name of Honey, at Caulfield Geriatric Hospital in Melbourne.

"Patients and staff were interviewed before the study about their attitudes and anticipations towards the dog and its presence in the hospital. For a period of about six months the dog was permitted to interact with patients," reports Eve.

"The results obtained clearly show that patients' expectations were more than realized. In addition, the staff experienced benefits as well. Honey opened lines of communication between them and the residents which had not been open previously.

"The ward took on a home-like atmosphere, there was more enjoyment, more interest and more socialization among the residents. Before Honey, the patients spent an average of sixteen hours a day alone. By the end of the program, the patients' time alone had been reduced to eleven hours a day."

From the human medical field, Michael McCulloch, M.D., reported how thirty-one pet-owning, medically ill, depressed outpatients were examined. The pets were felt to be an important source of companionship during illness by distracting patients from worries and making them feel needed.

"Affection, playfulness and helping to cope with loneliness and isolation," reports McCulloch, "were also important factors. The most prominent finding in the study was that the patients believed their pets helped them to laugh and maintain a sense of humor."

Drs. Alan Beck and Aaron Katcher reported how aquarium contemplation by dental patients lowered their blood pressure. And, interestingly, they reported on findings involving people when they talked to other people versus when they talked to their pets. Invariably, systolic blood pressure rose when they talked to other people and lowered when they talked to pets!

From the field of research, Dr. Stephen Kellert presented a report on the relationship between childhood cruelty to animals and aggressive behavior among criminals in adulthood. In addition he discussed the possible association of family violence, childhood/animal cruelty and aggressiveness toward humans in adults.

The data for this study were derived from personal interviews with criminals who were inmates at the federal penitentiaries in Leavenworth, Kansas, and Danbury, Connecticut, and noncriminals residing in the surrounding areas of Kansas and Connecticut.

Kellert reported, "The strength of the findings suggests that aggression among adult criminals may be strongly correlated with a history of family abuse and childhood cruelty toward animals. This data should alert researchers, clinicians, and societal leaders to the importance of childhood animal cruelty as a potential indicator of disturbed family relationships and future anti-social and aggressive behavior.

"The evolution of a more gentle and benign relationship in human society might, thus, be enhanced by our promotion of a more positive and nurturing ethic between children and animals."

From England, Peter Messent, DVM, discussed pet population and its relation to the pet-owner bond. He collected data regarding pet population in sixteen countries in the United Kingdom, Europe, Canada, Australia, Japan and the United States.

In the United States in 1982, for example, he found the human population to be 231 million. Of that number 42 percent of the people owned dogs and 26 percent of the people owned cats. Thus, the number of pet-owning people in the United States is a significant segment of the total population when you consider that these figures do not take into account people who own birds, fish and other pets. When all types of pets were considered, the percentage of households owning pets was significantly higher.

Comparing pet ownership by country, he found the United States to have the highest percentage of dogs per household. Messent also discovered in Austria, Norway and Switzerland there are more cat owners than dog owners. As far as dog owners are concerned, Australia was second to the United States with 39 percent, and France claims 35 percent of the population owning dogs.

In a paper titled "Applied Ethology in Dog Training" Dr. Torbjorn Owren from Norway explained, from the small animal practitioner's point of view, why veterinarians must expand their knowledge of dog behavior to encompass training and solving behavior problems.

"The human/companion animal bond concept has made us aware that the small animal practice is far more than just treating sick animals. New demands are being placed upon the veterinary profession. We now have to become involved in pet owner problems and the difficulties for the community at large arising from the keeping of pets. We have to give advice on raising, training and solving problems with dogs.

"This knowledge will not only help the owners and the public, but through the vet's interest and involvement in these fields, he will be regarded as a better practitioner. In other words, knowledge of ethology will make your practice grow."

From the contents of the Lorenz Symposium it seems obvious the pursuit of study in the human/pet science has, some thirty years after Konrad Lorenz pioneered this ethological interest, become a reality. As Dr. Katcher stated in 1982, the role of pets in today's world is an ambiguous one.

We regard them at different times in different ways, and the research into those times and ways has just begun. To date we know the potential for the future of man and animals is both promising and challenging if only we will recognize and embrace it.

Directory

DOG SPORTS

American Working Terrier Trials

JoAnn Frier
RD 3, Box 387
Robbinsville, New Jersey 08691

Karla Martin
9 Sunset Drive
Voorhees, New Jersey 08043

Back Packing

Alan Riley
6315 N.E. 196th Street
Seattle, Washington 98155

The Tacoma Mountain Rescue Unit
Post Office Box 696
Tacoma, Washington 98401
(for back packing equipment)

Breed

American Kennel Club
51 Madison Avenue
New York, New York 10010

Companions: Pets/Buying a Pure-bred Dog

American Kennel Club
51 Madison Avenue
New York, New York 10010

Dog Sledding

International Sled Dog Racing Association
Donna Hawley
Post Office Box 446
Nordham, Idaho 83848

LaBetta Carhart
Bryrnwood Kennels
Warners Road
Mount Holly, New Jersey 08060

Larry Freas
Lar-Anne Dog Training School
182 Haddon Avenue
West Berlin, New Jersey 08009

Exhibition Teams

Arner Publications, Inc.
Post Office Box 307, Graves Road
Westmoreland, New York 13490

Field Trials

See *Breed*

Lure Coursing

American Sighthound Field Association

Mr. Gary Forrester
2050 Thelon Drive
York, Pennsylvania 17404

Leigh Littleton, Corresponding Secretary
5717 South Maryland
Chicago, Illinois 60637

Bunny Reed
RR 3
Ogden, Iowa 50212

Mr. Arnold Ross
4333 Mt. Jeffers Avenue
San Diego, California 92117

Obedience

National Association of Dog Obedience Instructors
Connie C. Ellis
219-26th Avenue S.W.
Vero Beach, Florida 32960

Scent Hurdle Racing

Scent Hurdle Races
Mr. Herbert Wegner
2202 Los Amigos Street
La Canada, California 91011

Peg Forte
Box 315, RD 1
Sliker Road
Glen Gardner, New Jersey 08826

Schutzhund

The North American Working Dog Association
George Theriot
7318 Brennans Drive
Dallas, Texas 75214

Stock Dog Trials

All Breed Trial Association
Henry Trusler
Post Office Box 476
Roy, Washington 98580

Tracking

Buckeye Tracking Club
Joyce Klamut
Box 323, Route 1
Dover, Ohio 44622

Lenape Tracking Club
Fran Wilmeth
294 Aquetong Road
New Hope, Pennsylvania 18938

Water Rescue

Mrs. George McDonnell
150 Sunset Avenue
Ridgewood, New Jersey 07450

THERAPY DOGS

Aged

Nursing Homes/Institutions/Hospitals

ORGANIZATIONS

California

The Latham Foundation
Latham Plaza Building
Clement and Schiller Streets
Alameda, California 94501

Riverside Humane Society
5791 Fremont
Riverside, California 92504

Monterey County S.P.C.A.
Post Office Box 3058
Monterey, California 93940

Colorado

Humane Society of the Pikes Peak Region
Post Office Box 187
Colorado Springs, Colorado 80901

Hawaii

Hawaiian Humane Society
2700 Waialae Avenue
Honolulu, Hawaii 96822

Illinois

The Anti-Cruelty Society
Robert A. Brown
157 West Grand Avenue
Chicago, Illinois 60610

Indiana

People and Animals Together
Lynne A. Murray
St. Vincent Stress Center
Post Office Box 40970
Indianapolis, Indiana 46240-0970

Massachusetts

Junior League of Boston
Mrs. Henry Phillips Williams
476 Concord Road
Weston, Massachusetts 02193

Retirement Center of Wright County
200 Park Lane
Buffalo, Minnesota 55313

New Jersey

Therapy Dogs International
Elaine Smith
1536 Morris Place
Hillside, New Jersey 07205

New York

Bide-A-Wee Association
3300 Beltagh Avenue
Wantagh, New York 11793

Washington

The Delta Society
Dr. Leo K. Bustad, President
N.E. 1705 Upper Drive
Pullman, Washington 99163

People-Pet Partnership Program
Linda Hines, Director
Spillman Hall 148
College of Veterinary Medicine
Washington State University
Pullman, Washington 99164-6012

INDIVIDUALS

Alabama

Jackie Kirkland
1009 Queensbury Road
Birmingham, Alabama

California

Susan Myles
502 31st Street
Newport Beach, California 92663

Maryland

Dr. James Lynch
Psychophysiological Clinic & Laboratories
University of Maryland School of Medicine
655 West Baltimore Street
Baltimore, Maryland 21201

Pennsylvania

Dr. Alan Beck
Center on the Interactions of Animals and Society
School of Veterinary Medicine
University of Pennsylvania
3800 Spruce Street
Philadelphia, Pennsylvania 19104
(conducts research, provides behavioral services, and works with veterinary students to further understanding of the bond between people and pets)

Dr. Daniel Lago
Gerontology Center
Pennsylvania State University
State College, Pennsylvania

Washington

Terry Ryan
N.W. 2025 Friel Street
Pullman, Washington 99163

Australia

Judy Hubbard
Honorary Secretary
JACOPIS
117 Collins Street
Melbourne, 3000, Australia

Canada

Dr. Sheilah Fletch
Sunnybrook Medical Centre
Toronto, Canada

Veterinary Related Subjects

ORGANIZATIONS

California

California Veterinary Medical Association
Ilka Wood
1024 Country Club Drive
Moraga, California 94556

The Latham Foundation
Latham Plaza Building
Clement and Schiller Streets
Alameda, California 94501
(encourages respect to all life through education)

"Pet by Rx"
Joan Schaeffler, DVM
Contra Costa County Veterinary Medical Association
24 Meese Circle
Danville, California 54526

Minnesota

CENSHARE (Center to Study Human/Animal Relationships and Environments)
1-117 Health Science Unit A
University of Minnesota
Minneapolis, MN 55455
(serves as an information clearinghouse for individuals pursuing research on the H/CAB)

Washington, D.C.

Scientists Center for Animal Welfare
Post Office Box 3755
Washington, D.C. 20007
(dedicated to advancing scientific knowledge about animals including the ethical aspects of human-animal relationships)

INDIVIDUALS

Minnesota

Dr. R.K. Anderson
1360 Mayo Building
University of Minnesota
Minneapolis, MN 55455
(a report prepared by the School of Public Health: *Description of the Responsibilities of Veterinarians as They Relate Directly to Human Health*)

Texas

Dr. William McCulloch
AVMA's H/CAB–Animal Welfare Committee
Texas A & M University
College Station, Texas 77843

Washington

Dr. Marie Zeglen, Biomedical Communications
Washington State University
Pullman, Washington 99164-6021
(*Optimal Placement of Pets with The Institutionalized Elderly*)

Autistic Children

INDIVIDUALS

Sue Myles
502 31st Street
Newport Beach, California 92663

Cheryl Rahaman
RD 3, Box 381
New Paltz, New York 12561

Handicapped

ORGANIZATIONS

Arizona

Alamo Reaves
Handi-Dogs, Inc.
Post Office Box 12563
Tucson, Arizona 85732

California

Canine Companions for Independence
Post Office Box 446
Santa Rosa, California 95402

The Latham Foundations
Latham Plaza Building
Clement and Schiller Streets
Alameda, California 94501

Gerald Jay Westbrook
University of Southern California
Gerontology Center - 213
Los Angeles, California 90089-0192

Pennsylvania

Mrs. Everett S. Hayes
Aid Dogs for the Handicapped Foundation
1312 Bergan Road
Oreland, Pennsylvania 19075

Washington

Dr. Leo K. Bustad, President
The Delta Society
N.E. 1705 Upper Drive
Pullman, Washington 99163

Linda Hines, Director
People-Pet Partnership Program
Spillman Hall 148
College of Veterinary Medicine
Washington State University
Pullman, Washington 99164-6012

INDIVIDUALS

California

Sue Myles
Able Dogs
502 31st Street
Newport Beach, California 92663

New Hampshire

Gail T. Fisher
Box 64A, Canterbury Road
Northwood, New Hampshire 03261

New Jersey

Charlotte Schwartz
Brandy Lane Training School
RD 2, Box 2142
Mount Holly, New Jersey 08060

Washington

Terry Ryan
N.W. 2025 Friel Street
Pullman, Washington 99163

Hearing Ear

ORGANIZATIONS

California

Canine Companions for Independence
Post Office Box 446
Santa Rosa, California 95402

Hearing Dog Program
The San Francisco Society for the Prevention of Cruelty to Animals
2500 16th Street
San Francisco, California 94103

Colorado

The American Humane Association
9725 East Hampden Avenue
Denver, Colorado
(dedicated to the prevention of cruelty to children and animals. Actively involved in hearing dog placement)

Hearing Dogs Inc.
5901 East 89th Avenue
Henderson, Colorado 80640
(trains and places dogs for the hearing-impaired)

International Hearing Dog, Inc.
5901 East 89th Avenue
Henderson, Colorado 80640

Connecticut

Hearing Ear Dogs of New England, Ltd.
420 Groton Long Point Road
Groton, Connecticut 06340

Florida

Hearing Ear Dog Program
Ms. Jean Warren
Post Office Box 15865
Southgate Station
Sarasota, Florida 33579

Maryland

Hearing Ear Dog Program
Mrs. Joan T. Adler
14238 Briarwood Terrace
Rockville, Maryland 20853

Massachusetts

Hearing Ear Dog Program
Ms. Shelley MacDonald
57 Dean Street
Attleboro, Massachusetts 02705

Hearing Ear Dog Program
Bryant Hill Farm
Jefferson, Massachusetts 01522

Red Acre Farm, Hearing Dog Center
Box 278
109 Red Acre Road
Stow, Massachusetts 01775

New Hampshire

Hearing Ear Dog Program
Mrs. Sally Martel
West Street
Antrim, New Hampshire 03440

New York

Hearing Dogs for the Deaf, Inc.
Putnam, New York

Assistance Dogs International, Inc.
527 Madison Avenue
New York, New York 10022

North Carolina

Hearing Ear Dog Program
Ms. Alice Baxter
130 North Ashe
Southern Pines, North Carolina 28287

Oregon

Roy G. Kabat, Director
Dogs for the Deaf
13260 Highway 238
Jacksonville, Oregon 97530

Pennsylvania

Hearing Ear Dog Program
Ms. Sandra K. Breman
1410 Barnsdale Street
Pittsburgh, Pennsylvania 15217

Wyoming

Hearing Ear Dog Program
Ms. Anita Nichols
920 North Main Street
Sheridan, Wyoming 82801

INDIVIDUALS

California

Sue Myles
502 31st Street
Newport Beach, California 92663

New Jersey

Charlotte Schwartz
Brandy Lane Farm
RD 2, Box 2142
Mount Holly, New Jersey 08055

Washington

Terry Ryan
N.W. 1025 Friel Street
Pullman, Washington 99163

England

P.R. Messent, Animal Behaviorist
Freeby Lane
Waltham-on-the-Wolds
Melton Mowbray
Leicestershire LE144RT
England

INDIVIDUALS

Cheryl Rahaman
RD 3, Box 381
New Paltz, New York 12561

Prisons

INDIVIDUALS

David Lee
Lima State Hospital for Criminally Insane
Lima, Ohio

Kathy Quinn
Purdy Prison Therapy Program
Washington State University
Pullman, Washington 99164-6021

Seeing Eye

ORGANIZATIONS

California

Guide Dogs for the Blind
Post Office Box 1200
San Rafael, California 94915

International Guiding Eyes
2221 Empire
Burbank, California 91603

Michigan

Leader Dogs for the Blind
1039 South Rochester Road
Rochester, Michigan 48063

New Jersey

Seeing Eye
Post Office Box 375M
Washington Valley Road
Morristown, New Jersey 07960

New York

Guide Dog Foundation for the Blind, Inc.
109-19 72nd Avenue
Forest Hills, New York 11375

Guiding Eyes for the Blind
Yorktown Heights, New York 10598

Ohio

Pilot Dogs
625 West Town Street
Columbia, Ohio 43215

Additional Therapy Dog Material

For *Bibliography of Published Material and Reprints on the Human/Companion Animal Bond* write to:

The Latham Foundation
Latham Plaza Building
Clement and Schiller Streets
Alameda, California 94501

For *Pet Therapy: A Study of the Use of Companion Animals in Selected Therapies,* by Phil Arkow, write to:

The Humane Society of the Pikes Peak Region
633 South 8th Street
Post Office Box 187
Colorado Springs, Colorado 80901
(copies are available at $10 each plus $1.50 handling)

SERVICE DOGS

Bovine Estrus

ORGANIZATIONS

H.W. Hawk
Reproduction Laboratory
Animal Physiology & Genetics Institute
USDA, SEA
Beltsville, Maryland 20705

Daniel S. Mitchell, Ph.D.
Department of Bioengineering, Behavioral Science
Southwest Research Institute
6220 Culebra Road
San Antonio, Texas 78284

INDIVIDUALS

Dan Barker
360 Lightner Street
State College, Pennsylvania 16801

Glenn Johnson
Guardian Training Academy
RR 1
Oldcastle, Ontario
Nor ILO, Canada

Earl Ryba
Fahracres
Julian, Pennsylvania 16844

Deer Search

John R. Jeanneney
Clinton Corners Road
Clinton Corners, New York 12541

Earthquakes

ORGANIZATIONS

Project Earthquake Watch
Post Office Box 295
Stanford, California 94305

Herding/Guarding

Herding: General

ORGANIZATIONS

The National Stock Dog Registry
Route 1
Butler, Indiana 46721

All Breed Trial Association
Henry Trusler
Post Office Box 476
Roy, Washington 98580

INDIVIDUALS

Mr. Ed Emmanuel
Route 1
Butler, Indiana 46721

Herding: Breeds

ORGANIZATIONS

Australian Cattle Dogs

Working Cattle Dog Council
Box 390
San Marcos, California 92069

Australian Shepherds

Australian Shepherd Club of America
Lisa Ford
Route 3, Box 612
College Station, Texas 77840

Bearded Collie

Bearded Collie Club of America
Nancy Winter
Route 1, Box 208
Waconia, Minnesota 55387

Border Collie

North American Sheep Dog Society
210 East Main Street
McLeansboro, Illinois 62859

Catahoula Leopard Cowdog

National Association of Louisiana Catahoula Leopard Cowdogs
Box 1041
Denham Springs, Louisiana 70726

Cur
Howard Carnathon
Route 1, Box 185
Deatsville, Alabama 36022

English Shepherds
The English Shepherd Club
Diana Karr, Secretary
1251 Stevens Avenue
Arbutus, Maryland 21227

Kelpies
Robert Carrillo
3225 Bloomfield Road
Sebastopol, California 95472

Guarding: General

ORGANIZATIONS

Winrock International Livestock
Research and Training Center
Morrilton, Arkansas

Livestock Dog Project
Raymond and Lorna Coppinger
Chestnut Hill Road–RFD
Montague, Massachusetts 01351
(author of *Livestock Guarding Dogs for U.S. Agriculture*)

Guarding: Publication

The Guardian
c/o Patricia Edward
Rt. 3, Box 167
Birch Tree, Montana 65438

Guarding: Breeds

ORGANIZATIONS

Anatolian Akbash
The Anatolian Akbash Dog Club of America
5829 Marbury Road
Bethesda, Maryland 20034

Anatolian Shepherds
Anatolian Shepherd Dog Club of America
Post Office Box 1271
Alpine, California 92001

Great Pyrenees

Great Pyrenees Club of America
Mrs. Betty Wade, Secretary
3715 Dell Road
Carmichael, California 95608

Komondor

Komondor Club of America, Inc.
Mary Silkworth, Secretary
Post Office Box 455
Ypsilanti, Michigan 48197

Kuvasz

Kuvasz Club of America
A. Andres, Secretary
18 South Paris Avenue
Mount Vernon, New York 10550

Shar Planinetz

American Yugoslav Shepherd Dog Club
18335 Aguiro
Rowland Heights, California 91748

Narcotics and Bombs

INDIVIDUALS

Captain Arthur Haggerty
401 East 76th Street
New York, New York 10021

Glenn Johnson
Guardian Training Academy
RR 1
Oldcastle, Ontario
Nor IL0, Canada

Gerry Lapham
6595 Gooden Road
Sentinel K-9 School
Fayetteville, North Carolina

Carl Rickert
BJR Private Investigation and Security Service
Plaza 82, Suite Three, Box 333
Gainesville, Texas 76240

Kathy Uhrman
Bridlewold, N. Bella Bridge Road
Medford, New Jersey 08055

GOVERNMENT AGENCIES

United States Police Canine Association, Inc.
8616 Trumps Hill Road
Upper Marlboro, Maryland 20772

United States Customs Service
Canine Enforcement Training Center
RR 22, Box 7
Front Royal, Virginia 22630

Olfactory Specialists

INSTITUTIONS

Department of Physiology
School of Medicine
University of Pennsylvania and
Veterans Administration Hospital
Philadelphia, Pennsylvania 19104

ORGANIZATIONS

Buckeye Tracking Club
Joyce Klamut
Box 323, Route 1
Dover, Ohio 44622

Lenape Tracking Club
Fran Wilmeth
294 Aquetong Road
New Hope, Pennsylvania 18938

INDIVIDUALS

Glenn Johnson
Guardian Training Academy
RR 1
Oldcastle, Ontario
Nor IL0, Canada

Mildred E. Rothrock
8439 Elphick Road
Sebastopol, California 95472

W. Herbert Morrison
2126 White Oak Drive
Athens, Georgia 30606

Earl Ryba
Fahracres
Julian, Pennsylvania 16844

Charlotte Schwartz
Brandy Lane Farm
RD 2, Box 2142
Mount Holly, New Jersey 08060

Edwin Wight
Box 379
Clinton, Michigan 49236

Mr. Richard O. Zerbe
729 Evergreen Drive
Akron, Ohio 44303

Police K-9

United States Police Canine Association, Inc.
8616 Trumps Hill Road
Upper Marlboro, Maryland 20772

Search and Rescue

NATIONAL ORGANIZATIONS

American Rescue Dog Association
Alice Stanley, Secretary
Route 1, Box 161-K
Woodford, Virginia 22580
National Search Alert: 206-282-1177

National Association for Search and Rescue
Post Office Box 2123
LaJolla, California 92038

National Police Bloodhound Association
Box 43, Dewart, Pennsylvania 17730
Search Alert: 717-538-9001

ORGANIZATIONS

Alaska

Dogs Organized for Ground Search
SRA Box 2064
Anchorage, Alaska 99507
Search Alert: 907-344-1329

Southeast Alaska Dogs Organized for Ground Search
Post Office Box 244
Juneau, Alaska 99802
Search Alert: 907-465-4310

California

Sonoma County Sheriff's Search and Rescue
Jim Murphy
900 Gravenstein Hwy. No.
Sebastopol, California 95472
Search Alert: 707-823-7614

Woof Search Dog Unit
Marin County Sheriff's Department
Civic Center
San Rafael, California 94903
Search Alert: 415-499-7243

Illinois

Illini Search and Rescue Service, Inc.
1106 South Fern Drive
Mount Prospect, Illinois 60056
Search Alert: 312-640-0102

Massachusetts

New England K-9 Search and Rescue
Richard A. Dennis
Parker Road, Rt. 2
Shirley, Massachusetts 01464

Minnesota

Minnesota Search and Rescue Dog Association
Charles Ek
21768 Zumbroto Street N.E.
Cedar, Minnesota 55011
Search Alert: 612-434-7709

New Jersey

Ramapo Rescue Dog Association
247 Airmount Avenue
Ramsey, New Jersey 07446
Search Alert: 201-664-1111

New Mexico

Albuquerque Rescue Dog Association
Margaret Lilley
572 Berry Road N.W.
Albuquerque, New Mexico 87107

New York

Adirondack Rescue Dog Association, Inc.
Post Office Box 2125
Empire State Plaza Station
Albany, New York 12220
Search Alert: 518-462-6964

Palisades Search and Rescue Dog Association
Gene Schweikhard, Secretary
RD 1, Fran Road, Box 114
Goshen, New York 10924
Search Alert: 914-357-2400

Track Kennels Traildog Team
RD 2, 1512 Elm Street Ext.
Groton, New York 13073
Search Alert: 607-844-4007

Wilderness Volunteer Search and Rescue Team, Inc.
Post Office Box 770
Dryden, New York 13053
Search Alert: 607-844-4007

North Carolina

North Carolina Search and Rescue Dog Association, Inc.
Norma L. Davis
Route 3, Box 476
Waynesville, North Carolina 28786
Search Alert: 704-648-2351

Tar Hill Search and Rescue
Post Office Box 206
Canton, NC 28716
Search Alert: 704-648-2351

Pennsylvania

Pa. Wing—Civil Air Patrol
LTC Hubert J. Waskovich
Box 62
Drums, Pennsylvania 18222
Search Alert: 717-788-3382

Utah

Rocky Mountain Rescue Dogs, Inc.
John Pickup
55 West 1600 South
Orem, Utah 84057
Search Alert: 801-766-3060

Virginia

Dogs - East, Inc.
Post Office Box 344
Haymarket, Virginia 22069
Search Alert: 703-369-9468

Virginia Search and Rescue Dog Association
Post Office Box 141
Thornburg, Virginia 22565
Search Alert: 703-659-4131

Washington

Search and Rescue Dog Association for Washington
14253 130th Place N.E.
Kirkland, Washington 98033
Search Alert: 206-282-1177

Wisconsin

Headwaters Search and Rescue Dog Association, Inc.
Pioneer Lake
Conover, Wisconsin 54519
Search Alert: 715-479-4441

Wilderness Search and Rescue
Marie Nielson
Route 2, Box 434A
Ashland, Wisconsin 54806
Search Alert: 715-682-5595

United States Customs Service

GOVERNMENT AGENCIES

Department of the Treasury
United States Customs Service
Washington, D.C. 20229

BIBLIOGRAPHY

ALL OWNERS of pure-bred dogs will benefit themselves and their dogs by enriching their knowledge of breeds and of canine care, training, breeding, psychology and other important aspects of dog management. The following list of books covers further reading recommended by judges, veterinarians, breeders, trainers and other authorities. Books may be obtained at the finer book stores and pet shops, or through Howell Book House Inc., publishers, New York.

Breed Books

AFGHAN HOUND, Complete *Miller & Gilbert*
AIREDALE, New Complete *Edwards*
AKITA, Complete *Linderman & Funk*
ALASKAN MALAMUTE, Complete *Riddle & Seeley*
BASSET HOUND, Complete *Braun*
BEAGLE, New Complete *Noted Authorities*
BLOODHOUND, Complete *Brey & Reed*
BOXER, Complete *Denlinger*
BRITTANY SPANIEL, Complete *Riddle*
BULLDOG, New Complete *Hanes*
BULL TERRIER, New Complete *Eberhard*
CAIRN TERRIER, Complete *Marvin*
CHESAPEAKE BAY RETRIEVER, Complete *Cherry*
CHIHUAHUA, Complete *Noted Authorities*
COCKER SPANIEL, New *Kraeuchi*
COLLIE, New *Official Publication of the Collie Club of America*
DACHSHUND, The New *Meistrell*
DALMATIAN, The *Treen*
DOBERMAN PINSCHER, New *Walker*
ENGLISH SETTER, New Complete *Tuck, Howell & Graef*
ENGLISH SPRINGER SPANIEL, New *Goodall & Gasow*
FOX TERRIER, New Complete *Silvernail*
GERMAN SHEPHERD DOG, New Complete *Bennett*
GERMAN SHORTHAIRED POINTER, New *Maxwell*
GOLDEN RETRIEVER, New Complete *Fischer*
GORDON SETTER, Complete *Look*
GREAT DANE, New Complete *Noted Authorities*
GREAT DANE, The—Dogdom's Apollo *Draper*
GREAT PYRENEES, Complete *Strang & Giffin*
IRISH SETTER, New Complete *Eldredge & Vanacore*
IRISH WOLFHOUND, Complete *Starbuck*
KEESHOND, Complete *Peterson*
LABRADOR RETRIEVER, Complete *Warwick*
LHASA APSO, Complete *Herbel*
MINIATURE SCHNAUZER, Complete *Eskrigge*
NEWFOUNDLAND, New Complete *Chern*
NORWEGIAN ELKHOUND, New Complete *Wallo*
OLD ENGLISH SHEEPDOG, Complete *Mandeville*
PEKINGESE, Quigley Book of *Quigley*
PEMBROKE WELSH CORGI, Complete *Sargent & Harper*
POODLE, New Complete *Hopkins & Irick*
POODLE CLIPPING AND GROOMING BOOK, Complete *Kalstone*
ROTTWEILER, Complete *Freeman*
SAMOYED, Complete *Ward*
SCHIPPERKE, Official Book of *Root, Martin, Kent*
SCOTTISH TERRIER, New Complete *Marvin*
SHETLAND SHEEPDOG, The New *Riddle*
SHIH TZU, Joy of Owning *Seranne*
SHIH TZU, The (English) *Dadds*
SIBERIAN HUSKY, Complete *Demidoff*
TERRIERS, The Book of All *Marvin*
WEST HIGHLAND WHITE TERRIER, Complete *Marvin*
WHIPPET, Complete *Pegram*
YORKSHIRE TERRIER, Complete *Gordon & Bennett*

Breeding

ART OF BREEDING BETTER DOGS, New *Onstott*
BREEDING YOUR OWN SHOW DOG *Seranne*
HOW TO BREED DOGS *Whitney*
HOW PUPPIES ARE BORN *Prine*
INHERITANCE OF COAT COLOR IN DOGS *Little*

Care and Training

DOG OBEDIENCE, Complete Book of *Saunders*
NOVICE, OPEN AND UTILITY COURSES *Saunders*
DOG CARE AND TRAINING FOR BOYS AND GIRLS *Saunders*
DOG NUTRITION, Collins Guide to *Collins*
DOG TRAINING FOR KIDS *Benjamin*
DOG TRAINING, Koehler Method of *Koehler*
DOG TRAINING Made Easy *Tucker*
GO FIND! Training Your Dog to Track *Davis*
GUARD DOG TRAINING, Koehler Method of *Koehler*
OPEN OBEDIENCE FOR RING, HOME AND FIELD, Koehler Method of *Koehler*
STONE GUIDE TO DOG GROOMING FOR ALL BREEDS *Stone*
SUCCESSFUL DOG TRAINING, The Pearsall Guide to *Pearsall*
TOY DOGS, Kalstone Guide to Grooming All *Kalstone*
TRAINING THE RETRIEVER *Kersley*
TRAINING YOUR DOG—Step by Step Manual *Volhard & Fisher*
TRAINING YOUR DOG TO WIN OBEDIENCE TITLES *Morsell*
TRAIN YOUR OWN GUN DOG, How to *Goodall*
UTILITY DOG TRAINING, Koehler Method of *Koehler*
VETERINARY HANDBOOK, Dog Owner's Home *Carlson & Giffin*

General

AKC'S WORLD OF THE PURE-BRED DOG *American Kennel Club*
CANINE TERMINOLOGY *Spira*
COMPLETE DOG BOOK, The *Official Publication of American Kennel Club*
DOG IN ACTION, The *Lyon*
DOG BEHAVIOR, New Knowledge of *Pfaffenberger*
DOG JUDGE'S HANDBOOK *Tietjen*
DOG JUDGING, Nicholas Guide to *Nicholas*
DOG PEOPLE ARE CRAZY *Riddle*
DOG PSYCHOLOGY *Whitney*
DOGSTEPS, Illustrated Gait at a Glance *Elliott*
DOG TRICKS *Haggerty & Benjamin*
ENCYCLOPEDIA OF DOGS, International *Dangerfield, Howell & Riddle*
FROM RICHES TO BITCHES *Shattuck*
IN STITCHES OVER BITCHES *Shattuck*
JUNIOR SHOWMANSHIP HANDBOOK *Brown & Mason*
MY TIMES WITH DOGS *Fletcher*
OUR PUPPY'S BABY BOOK (blue or pink)
SUCCESSFUL DOG SHOWING, Forsyth Guide to *Forsyth*
TRIM, GROOM & SHOW YOUR DOG, How to *Saunders*
WHY DOES YOUR DOG DO THAT? *Bergman*
WILD DOGS in Life and Legend *Riddle*
WORLD OF SLED DOGS, From Siberia to Sport Racing *Coppinger*